The Last Physician

THE LAST PHYSICIAN

Walker Percy and the Moral Life of Medicine

Edited by Carl Elliott and John Lantos

DUKE UNIVERSITY PRESS   Durham and London 1999

© 1999 Duke University Press

All rights reserved

Printed in the United States of America on acid-free paper ∞

Typeset in Stone Serif by Tseng Information Systems, Inc.

Library of Congress Cataloging-in-Publication Data appear

on the last printed page of this book.

Who of us is not so strangely alone that it is
the cool clinical touch of a stranger that serves
best to treat his aloneness?
—Walker Percy, *Love in the Ruins*

Contents

Acknowledgments

Several of the papers in this collection were first presented at a conference on Walker Percy at the University of Chicago's MacLean Center for Clinical Medical Ethics in 1995. We would like to thank Mrs. D. J. MacLean for her generous support of that conference, and Mark Siegler for his help in organizing it. We are grateful to Miriam Angress and Reynolds Smith at Duke University Press for their editorial help. Rachel Toor deserves special thanks for going beyond the call of duty in helping us bring the book to completion.

John Lantos would like to thank Anne Dudley Goldblatt for many hours of discussion on literature and medicine. Carl Elliott would like to thank Robert Crouch for his excellent research assistance. This research was supported by grants from Fonds pour la Formation de Chercheurs et l'Aide à la Recherche and the Social Science and Humanities Research Council of Canada.

The Last Physician

Introduction

Carl Elliott

I was not an enthusiastic medical student. For most of my four years at the Medical University of South Carolina I resembled a clinician-in-training less than I resembled a chronic patient on the locked psychiatric ward. On better days I was depressed. Other days I paced back and forth between hospitals, head down, muttering obscenities about my professors under my breath. What exactly had I expected of medical school? An intellectual adventure? Like-minded classmates? Selfless teachers inspiring reverence for the nobility of the profession? As Bogart says to Claude Raines in *Casablanca:* I was misinformed. I felt as if I had landed on an alien planet. The landscape looked grim, the inhabitants desperate. On my first day, a sweltering Low-Country afternoon in August, I got stuck for three hours in a broken hospital elevator with ten agitated, sweating medical students. Medical school went downhill from there.

Maybe you have come across a book you feel must have been written precisely with you in mind. By this I mean a book that comes at exactly the right time and place and not only speaks to you but also speaks *for* you, that gives a voice to your own unarticulated, half-formed ideas. For me that book was Walker Percy's *The Moviegoer.* I was midway through my third year of medical school when Daniel Fort, a Sewanee Episcopalian who was almost as depressed and alienated by medical school as I was, handed me a paperback copy, shook his head, and said, "Here, read this. A few years ago it really fucked me up. But in a good way." The book astonished me. As Percy himself might have put it: I felt like Robinson Crusoe seeing footprints on the beach. A fellow castaway! Binx Bolling's predicament sounded exactly like mine, maybe even worse. Yet up to that point, I could not even have told you what that predicament was. All I knew was that despite being a southerner, I didn't feel much like the cheerful southerners who surrounded me; that despite heading full steam toward a medical career, I didn't especially envy or admire doctors; that in fact, I was even beginning to have my doubts about the whole American project, the pursuit of happiness, which seemed to require not only that I pursue happiness but that I pursue it aggressively, club it into unconsciousness, and drag it back bound and gagged to my basement.

Most of all I felt detached from my fellow medical students. While they intently percussed chests and drew blood gases and memorized the most common presentations for an inguinal hernia all I could think was, Good Lord, is this it? Poking your nose in strangers' mouths and feeling their genitalia? It might be possible to spend one's entire life taking vital signs without once attending to the puzzle of life and death. I felt more like Binx, who looks over at his lab partner and says, "I wouldn't trade places with him if he discovered the causes and cure of cancer. He is no more aware of the mystery that surrounds him than a fish is aware of the water it swims in. He could do research for a thousand years and never have an inkling of it."

I can remember reading one passage from *The Moviegoer* so often that I could recite it, a passage in which Percy seemed to have put his finger precisely on my own condition, a condition Binx calls the malaise, or, as he describes it, "the pain of loss. The world is lost to you, the world and the people in it, and there remains only you and the world and you no more able to be in the world than Banquo's ghost." In that passage, Binx tells of a trip to the beach with his girlfriend Marcia in his new Dodge sedan, a perfect car that despite its perfection, or perhaps because of it, becomes a "regular incubator of malaise."

> Though it was comfortable enough, though it ran like a clock, though we went spinning along in perfect comfort and with a perfect view of the scenery like the American couple in the Dodge ad, the malaise quickly became suffocating. We sat frozen in gelid amiability. Our cheeks ached from smiling. Either would have died for the other. In despair I put my hand under her dress, but even such a homely little gesture as that was received with the same fearful politeness. I longed to stop the car and bang my head against the curb.

Exactly! And yet when I read this passage for the first time, a remarkable thing happened. I felt immediately better. How extraordinary! There I sat, a medical student just this side of clinical depression reading a book about the everydayness of modern life, a book whose narrator speaks dryly about the despair and malaise of the modern age and whose author professed to require five shots of Early Times just to get through an ordinary Wednesday afternoon, and my spirits lifted. Yet when I looked around at my fellow South Carolinians—prosperous folk most of them, living in Charleston, the

South's loveliest city, as satisfied as channel catfish and no more perturbed about their place in the world—I felt like hurling myself into the Cooper River. Clearly, something strange was going on here.

The standard book jacket biography of Walker Percy usually goes something like this: "Percy was educated at the University of North Carolina and at Columbia University, where he received his M.D. in 1941. After several months of internship in pathology at Bellevue Hospital, he contracted tuberculosis and spent the next three years recovering from his illness. He then married Mary Bernice Townsend, converted to Catholicism, and became a writer, first of essays, then of fiction. His first published novel, *The Moviegoer,* won the National Book Award in 1962. His other published novels are *The Last Gentleman, Love in the Ruins, Lancelot, The Second Coming,* and *The Thanatos Syndrome.* His nonfiction books are *The Message in the Bottle, Lost in the Cosmos,* and a posthumous collection of essays, *Signposts in a Strange Land.* He lived in Covington, Louisiana, until his death in 1990."

A thumbnail biography does not do justice even to an ordinary life, much less to one as quietly extraordinary as Percy's: the distinguished southern family into which he was born; the suicides of his father and grandfather; the mysterious death of his mother in a car accident; his and his two brothers' adoption by their cousin, the poet, lawyer, and planter Will Percy; the years he spent in sanitoriums recovering from his tuberculosis; his internal struggles with the family legacy of suicide and depression. But even the bare outlines of Percy's life make it clear that he was a writer more familiar than most with illness and its treatment. Doctors who turn to writing are by no means unheard of—Keats, Chekhov, Maugham, Conan Doyle, William Carlos Williams—but a southern doctor who starts writing novels and philosophical essays after two years lying flat on his back in a TB sanitorium is a somewhat rarer bird.

Walker Percy is sometimes called a doctor-writer, but to tell the truth, a lot of doctors don't much take to his writing. Unlike, say, William Carlos Williams, or Richard Selzer, Percy doesn't write directly about the practice of medicine. His novels often concern doctors and patients, and the plots sometimes revolve around hospitals and clinics, but medical practice itself is often not so much the book's feature attraction as it is a convenient backdrop. Percy knows the culture of medicine like he knows the South, and he uses them both to great comic effect, but more often than not they seem rather incidental to his larger purposes.

Many physicians wouldn't consider Percy a real doctor, or even an ex-doctor. He never treated patients as a licensed physician; as a pathology intern, he mainly performed autopsies on the corpses of alcoholics. For some doctors, especially those in various stages of disillusionment with the profession, this may be part of Percy's appeal; as he once said, "I was the happiest man ever to contract tuberculosis, because it enabled me to get out of Bellevue and quit medicine."[1] His novels often portray medicine as a profession in decline, sold out to greedy capitalists and narrow scientists. The most appealing doctors in the novels are often burned-out and dispirited; the worst of them are quacks or crooks. Even the decent ones are often vaguely comical figures, like the husky Dr. Vance Battle of *The Second Coming,* a GP who likes nothing better than to "mend bones, take hold of your liver from front and back, stick a finger up your anus paying no attention to your groans, talking NC basketball all the while, pausing only to frown and shake his head at the state of one's prostate: 'It feels like an Idaho potato.'"

Yet Percy's experience as a doctor and a patient shows through in more subtle ways, and perhaps ultimately more important ones. It shows through in the doctorly way that Percy writes, for example—the wry, clinical detachment with which he describes his characters and the circumstances in which they find themselves. Percy's style is reminiscent of the way doctors often describe their patients: sometimes with affection, occasionally with condescension, often with humor—but always with an eye toward diagnosing their particular pathology. Percy himself described it as "the stance of a diagnostician."

> The physician-novelist is not in the business of writing edifying tales. He has other fish to fry. It is enough for him to have discovered and put his finger on the peculiar lesion of the age. Perhaps by this very act the abscess is lanced, the ear drained so that the patient, whatever else he might do, can at least hear. Nevertheless the physican, insofar as he is a novelist, is in the business of diagnosis, not therapy.[2]

Percy's kind of diagnostic exercise is aimed not at physical illness, of course, but at the spiritual pathologies endemic among late-twentieth-century westerners. It is the kind of endeavor undertaken in *Love in the Ruins,* by Tom More, an old-fashioned "physician of the soul" whose lapsometer can diagnose all manner of existential ailments. If anything marks Percy as a writer, it is this remarkable ability to diagnose what ails a certain kind of person: one who feels strangely lost in the world. Such a person, on reading Percy's novels, becomes convinced that the physician-writer has somehow found the lesion, diagnosed the disease, put his finger on the predicament.

Such a person is apt to ask the question that Ross McElwee asked after reading *The Last Gentleman:* "How was it that Percy happened to have known enough about me to have written my psychological biography?"

The answer may be that Percy is less a doctor-writer than a patient-writer, someone who knows what it is like to be sick. Certainly the heroes of Percy's novels are more often patients than doctors. *The Last Gentleman*'s Will Barrett lapses into fugue states and is apt to wake up to find himself hugging a tombstone on an old Confederate battleground. Allie Huger, Will's love in *The Second Coming,* is an escapee from a North Carolina mental institution who lives in an abandoned greenhouse. Lance Lamar narrates *Lancelot* from what appears to be a cell in a prison hospital or a facility for the criminally insane. Even Dr. Tom More spends less time on the psychiatric ward as a practitioner than he does as an inmate. Most afternoons he spends in his office with his feet up on the desk, drinking bourbon, watching the martins out the back door.

The essays collected in this volume center on the idea that, to paraphrase Brock Eide, there is profit to be had in thinking about Walker Percy as a physician, in a way that there is not in, say, thinking of T. S. Eliot as a banker. The essayists circle around these two subjects, Percy and medicine, and approach them in very distinctive ways. Some examine the ways in which Percy's writing reflects his training as a doctor. Others are more concerned with Percy's experience as a patient. Many see in Percy's novels and essays ideas that are important for medical practice and medical education, especially in psychiatry. Quite a few of the essayists are doctors themselves. Many strike a very personal tone, in some cases because the writers knew Percy, but also, I suspect, because of the deeply personal nature of Percy's writing.

Perhaps the most surprising thing about the essays, given that so many of the essayists are doctors, is the ambivalence toward medicine that often emerges—an ambivalence that Percy seemed to share, as Jay Tolson and Robert Coles point out. Most of the essays concern medicine in one form or another, but the image that is conveyed doesn't much resemble the heroic portrayal of doctors and medical science current in the popular media. Many of the essays communicate something very close to melancholy, a dimly felt sense that medicine is at the end of an era, caught up in forces beyond its control. What is being left behind is something that science doesn't capture, and economists can't measure, something that is often gestured at by the worn-out phrase "the art of medicine." Too often the result for doctors seems to be the feeling that David Schiedermayer describes, the disconcerting sense that he is "the last guardian of the Hippocratic Corpus."

Yet Schiedermayer may not be too far off the mark. If John Lantos's prediction turns out to be right—that with the rise of scientific medicine, the art of medicine may be destined to go the way of the arts of astrology and alchemy—then we may well be seeing the last of the old-style physicians. The "physician of the soul" that Percy sometimes wistfully describes just may be the end of the line for a dying species.

The irony of medical school is that you read more sentences but remember fewer of them than in any other four-year period of your life. I can remember very little of what I read in medical school other than Walker Percy's books, which is a little odd, since those books were probably the only things I read on which I was not later tested. Yet Percy's books stayed with me through medical school well after my first startled reading of *The Moviegoer*.

Three memories:

Early Sunday morning on the obstetrics ward. I have been on call all night, but the ward has been quiet. The few women admitted during the night have all delivered their babies. My scut work is finished, and I am drinking a cup of coffee alone in the break room. On the table in front of me is an open copy of Percy's *The Message in the Bottle*. Suddenly I hear footsteps in the hall. I look up and see one of the obstetrics attendings, a little Duke-trained Napoleon temporarily exiled in Charleston, fists clenched by his side. He is vibrating like a hornet. He is furious—at me? Sweat starts to bead on my forehead. I feel as if I've been caught with a copy of *Playboy* magazine. My face flushes. I stammer something about how Percy was actually a doctor, fumbling desperately for some explanation why I am reading this book instead of my ob-gyn textbooks. He doesn't buy it. He has never heard of Walker-goddamn-Percy. He lectures me in a machine-gun staccato for five minutes on my dedication to medicine. I decide I do not want to go into obstetrics.

Psychiatry rounds on the detox ward at the VA Hospital. I am sitting on the bed of a six-foot-five-inch black man named Cooper. Cooper is an alcoholic. His life is a wreck. He has lost his job because of his drinking, and he is about to lose his wife as well. Not that the marriage wasn't shaky enough already: a black man from Indianapolis, married to a white schoolteacher, two small children at home, living in the Deep South. No wonder he is an alcoholic. Walterboro, South Carolina, is not the place for you, I feel like telling him. Neither is the VA detox ward, for that matter. Dignified, college-educated, he seems lost among these hard-eyed Vietnam vets, like a character from Tolstoy who has accidentally wandered into a Sam Peckinpah film. Had I noticed a familiar look in his eyes as I worked him up him on admission?

Three days ago, on an impulse, I had given him my paperback copy of *The Last Gentleman.* Now I was having second thoughts. Percy might make him even more depressed. Had I remembered to ask him about suicidal ideation when I took his history? I need not have worried. He understands the book. He quotes Thoreau to me, the line about most men leading lives of quiet desperation—but he laughs when he says it. Amen to that, I say. We both shake our heads ruefully.

Graduation day at the Medical University. I am sitting under a blistering sun with my classmates, listening to the commencement ceremonies. My family is here, including my father, who graduated from this medical school thirty years ago, and one of my younger brothers, who will graduate two years later. We have just heard a speech by the president of the university, an ex-dentist and former cabinet appointee in the Reagan administration, and now we are listening to the formal commencement address, which is being delivered not by a famous medical scientist, as is the custom at many medical schools, but by a famous sailor. For some reason, this vaguely pleases me: sitting among the palmettos at the South's oldest medical school listening to a Reaganite dentist and a rich sports celebrity. "Medicine is like a yacht race," the sailor tells us, "and you are the captains of the ship." A horsefly buzzes around his neck, threatening to light on his left ear. The dentist is grinning like a game show host.

Several weeks earlier, I had received a short note from Walker Percy, a reply to a letter I had sent him a number of months previously. My own letter was a little embarrassing, to be honest. I had written with some questions about the place of existentialist philosophy in his novels, but what I was really hoping for was some kind of approval for what I was planning to do. Which was, in effect, to give up medicine, leave the South, move to Scotland, and study philosophy. Not many other people seemed to think this was a very good idea. When I had told one of my psychiatry professors, he had recommended psychotherapy. Percy's note was more gratifying. He said that I should read Kierkegaard and Heidegger ("nearly impenetrable, but worth it"), and then in closing: "We need more philosophers." Close enough to approval for me. What use did I have for grinning dentists and this quiet South Carolina desperation?

As for whether Percy was right, a decade or so later, I am not inclined to say, except that he was right about Heidegger, who is indeed close to impenetrable. I tend to think that things have turned out well. The note, for which I have always been grateful, I prefer to think of not so much as edifying advice as what Binx Bolling would call a good kick in the ass—if, as Binx says, ass kicking is properly distinguished from edification.

Notes

1 Quoted in James Atlas, "An Interview with Walker Percy," in *Conversations with Walker Percy,* ed. Lewis A. Lawson and Victor A. Kramer (Jackson: University Press of Mississippi, 1985), 185.
2 Walker Percy, "The Physician as Novelist," in *Signposts in a Strange Land,* ed. Patrick Samway (New York: Farrar, Straus and Giroux, 1991), 195.

Dr. Percy's Hold on Medicine

Robert Coles

In 1960 I was a physician who had received some training in pediatrics, psychiatry, and child psychiatry, after which I'd gone to Mississippi to work at an air force hospital, courtesy of the "doctor's draft," as it was then called—we all had to give the country two years of our time and energy. I had thereby come to the South for the first time; I had been born, reared, and educated in New England. During that time, I continued my psychoanalytic training, begun up north, at the New Orleans Psychoanalytic Institute. There I met other doctors, other psychiatrists; but there I also met southerners—who taught me a lot about a region I was, I fear, rather quick to judge out of hand. There I would take part in my first discussion of *The Moviegoer*—a few months after it was published in 1961.

I was in analysis then, and also taking courses at the institute. One day, after an analytic session and before a seminar, I had supper, and afterward, an hour or so on my hands, I browsed through a bookstore on Canal Street in downtown New Orleans, Doubleday's (long gone). So doing, I spotted a novel whose title really got to me for personal reasons: I constantly "flicked out," as some of us put it, to the point that my analyst, noting not only the frequency but, as he put it, the way I would "use" movies, "immerse" myself in them, get "distracted" by them, had called me a "moviegoer," even as, of course, he had wanted to know why, why—the "defensive" purpose of such activity. If I wasn't so anxious to learn my reasons from him (and myself, talking with him), I most certainly was intent on exploring the matter through this book, which I bought and read eagerly, hungrily—in one gulp (evening), actually.

I didn't return to Boston after my tour of medical military duty was over. I stayed in New Orleans, began studying the effect of school desegregation there on the children who initiated it, and gradually slipped into an odd working life as a documentary observer and writer. In a way, such research was not the total accident it seemed to be (a consequence of an air force assignment that landed me near New Orleans, so that I witnessed firsthand what happened to those children). I had majored in English, written a thesis on William Carlos Williams, got to know him, and had thereby been inspired to go into medicine. I admired not only his poetry and fiction but his doctoring life, the way he evoked and rendered the hopes and worries of the men and women and children he came to know so well as a physician. It became such a privilege to be able to follow, at least in modest part, those giant footsteps—and during my early days of "fieldwork," I was lucky to have his (often tough) criticism as I tried to figure out how to convey in words what I was hearing, seeing.

I began to realized in the middle 1960s that I had also found another source of medical inspiration, so to speak—another physician whose way of looking at this world gave me plenty to consider. Dr. Percy was obviously different in many respects from Dr. Williams—the former never practiced medicine; the latter did so from his early twenties to his late sixties, almost a half century of constant concern for patients, many of them needy, vulnerable not only physically but socially and economically. Moreover, until old age beset him with an assortment of ailments, Dr. Williams had always been in robust health, whereas Dr. Percy had known a serious, even life-threatening illness, tuberculosis, in his late twenties. It is foolish, of course, to think that the experience of sickness, in and of itself, will guarantee in an aspiring physician a heightened understanding of how patients feel, a greater empathy toward them; but Williams himself once addressed this subject in a way that, years later, would have a bearing on Walker Percy's life as a person seriously ill, as well as on his later philosophical reflections on consciousness, on how our mind often works in the course of a day's activities: "I've never really been flat on my back for any great length of time: down-and-out with something that's given me the feeling—well, there's Keats' 'intimations of mortality' to describe it [that feeling]. Sure, I think I know how it goes for a lot of my patients. I try to put myself in their shoes—I use my imagination, and I've been observing sickness, what it does to folks, for many years, and I keep reading the [medical] journals and the textbooks. But I'm busy—the old story!—and plenty of times I'm way behind in my schedule, and something else is on my mind, and so I'm not really 'with' the patient I'm seeing. That [state of mind] can go on and on: you're treating patients, but you're not giving them your best—I mean really connecting with them. I guess any busy doctor will tell you that happens; but when you do connect, when you listen carefully and have a good talk with someone who's in trouble, in pain, and wants just that, a doctor who offers concern and understanding as well as a prescription—then you know the difference between going through the motions and really 'being there' for someone.'"

In a sense, what Williams said in a casual conversation about his ongoing medical life (to a young medical student wondering how to become a reasonably able physician) Percy tried to comprehend in the distanced but penetrating and suggestive manner of the essayist and novelist—the physician become metaphysician. Indeed, after I'd become so taken with *The Moviegoer* (the novel kept coming to my mind as an analysand in that Prytania Street office I visited five days a week), I realized that I'd already read an essay by the same Walker Percy who had become a novelist, and had even cut it out: "The Man on the Train," published in the mid-1950s in the *Partisan Review.* That essay is a prefiguration of sorts to all of Percy's fiction. A writer of obvious moral energy is struggling to convey a line of reasoning (and feeling) in such a way that the reader won't easily forget what has been read—an especially important and ironic objective, because the essay is, actually, concerned with just that matter: how readily we lose sight of so much that truly counts, become lost in a reflexic tide of minute-by-minute activity that becomes, in fact, the life we live.

I got to know Walker Percy personally in 1972—I had been writing for the *New Yorker* (that is, for William Shawn, its editor) for several years and had done a number of book reviews and a long profile of Erik H. Erikson, who had been an important psychoanalytic guide of mine. (I ended up teaching in his Harvard College class when I returned from the South in 1966, after finishing my research on school desegregation and being much involved with the civil rights movement.) When Mr. Shawn asked me about whom I'd next like to write, I immediately mentioned Walker Percy. I didn't get a quick yes, though—a brilliant but cautious editor wanted to read Percy's two novels, *The Moviegoer* and *The Last Gentleman,* and some of his essays, published in philosophical journals and quarterlies and in *Commonweal* (at the time, his published body of work). Several weeks later, well into the evening, an obviously excited Mr. Shawn called me, and in his usual terse but now charged voice said, "An enthusiastic yes on Percy." I loved that message, and its dual meaning: approval for the profile and a fan's declaration of affiliation.

No question, the Danish philosopher and theologian Søren Kierkegaard was Dr. Percy's great intellectual, moral, and spiritual guide throughout his writing career, and before that, during the years when he was sick, and right afterward, when he was trying to find some direction and purpose for himself—as he told the world on many and diverse occasions, and as I would often hear him say when we talked. Indeed, Kierkegaard came up almost immediately at my first meeting with Dr. Percy in April 1972. Fortunately, I'd been exposed to the demanding work of that idiosyncratic Danish writer by Perry Miller, my college teacher and thesis adviser, who had us read *Fear and Trembling* and, Lord spare us, *Either/Or*—and how we tried and tried to comprehend a "thinker" who was then (still, actually) obscure and hugely insistent, ironic, sardonic. It was Professor Miller who got me to attend to Dr. Williams's poetry (not in the early 1950s popular with Harvard's English professors, many of whom had a hard time being interested in the ordinary, even down-and-out life evoked in *Paterson,* and some of whom had a hard time reaching for humility in themselves, never mind understanding it in others); and, for sure, it was Miller who prepared me for Dr. Percy. I had boned up on Kierkegaard before I went to see the seer of Covington, as some of us called him, out of his sight and hearing distance; and so when, inevitably, "Søren" (as we'd often refer to him) came up as a subject, I was "sort of" prepared. I kept using that two-word phrase as we began our talks—a way of endlessly qualifying what I had to say about the gloomy yet humorous writer whom Percy knew by heart, it seemed. Once, actually, as I yet again said "sort of" in connection with an opinion I had about an aspect of the ever-intimidating *Either/Or,* Percy told me that he thought Søren would like my way of qualifying my thoughts, with respect to that book or anything else. At once, I demurred, an automatic response based on a full knowledge of my ignorance—but Walker, as I'd begun calling him (to my dizzying delight) nevertheless seemed impressed, pleased—and by then, he and Søren had, anyway, merged in my mind, and I could only let the matter drop when I seemed to be ahead.

Over the years, as I studied Percy's work and wrote about him in various ways and places, I kept going back in my mind to times spent with him; to the jazz we both enjoyed hearing (he had a great collection); to the novelists we discussed (Dostoyevsky, Tolstoy, Camus, Dickens); to the shared experience we remembered as medical students at "P&S" (Columbia's College of Physicians and Surgeons), and as residents on the same (tenth) floor of the school's dormitory, with the same view of the Hudson River, although our stays were fourteen years apart (he'd come there in the late 1930s, I'd arrived in the early 1950s); but most of all, to our conversations about Kierkegaard, and to a lesser extent, Gabriel Marcel, Karl Jaspers, and Martin Heidegger. "I owe Søren a lot—he's the architect of my writing life," Walker once said. In reply, I joked: "Sort of." He smiled at what he recognized as a bit of self-parody on my part, but now he was quick to insist that he wanted no qualifications: "It's all there, in Søren's books." No wonder I began my profile with Kierkegaard—even as I'd done with my piece on Erikson, who was of Danish ancestry, had read Kierkegaard before he'd read Freud, and had a similar (more secret, certainly less acknowledged) interest in essays such as "The Problem of Anxiety" and *Stages on Life's Way*.

Percy's first novel, *The Moviegoer*, starts with a dedication to his father's cousin, the poet William Alexander Percy, who became the adoptive parent of Walker and his brothers, Leroy and Phinizy, after their mother's death, which followed by two years their father's suicide. On the next page we read: "The specific character of despair is precisely this: it is unaware of being despair"—that from Søren's *The Sickness unto Death*. Throughout Percy's career as first an essayist, then a novelist who wrote occasional essays, he hearkened back to that book, that message, and by so doing, affirmed himself as a physician, one who was concerned with a particular kind of "sickness," and, yes, "death": the gravest kind of illness, whose consequences so often are a kind of death that precedes the moment of dying—the extended living death that passes for "life" among so many of us. Binx Bolling, surely Percy's best-known character, caught the imagination of many of us because his life, his mental maneuvers and strategies, was ever so familiar, yet brought us up sharp: that familiarity (with the moral stupor of "everydayness") had become worked into our daily lives all too unselfconsciously—a lack of awareness not at all like that described by Freud and his heirs. Indeed, it was Percy's shrewdly psychiatric sense, his clinical acuity, that discouraged him from imagining Binx as yet another twentieth-century "neurotic"; and it was Percy's talent and skill as a writer that enabled him (so the judges for the National Book Award for 1962 eloquently, pointedly, instructively averred) to shun "the mannerisms of the clinic" in favor of "an intimation of mortality," a lovely way, indeed, of describing a book, and one that connects one writer who aspired to be a physician and suffered from tuberculosis, John Keats, with another whose life, in those respects, was similar.

Once, after a long time together talking of his novels, Percy suggested that I think again about the epigraph for his first novel, whereupon I recited it from memory. He smiled and said: "That's my hold on medicine. I'm trying to be a diagnostician who makes a little sense out of a malaise, a disease, or rather, a dis-ease that influences our lives more than we care to—dare to—realize, admit to ourselves, never mind anyone else." It was then that I remember thinking of him as more than Dr. Percy by virtue of his graduation from a medical school—rather, as Dr. Percy taking the measure of our collective distress, however set aside in our cleverly distracting minds, and rendering in essays and fiction the nature of that disorder, its symptoms, and, not least, its etiology. Moreover, by implication, he offers the obvious, if often hard-to-secure, "treatment plan," the I-Thou of "existentialism," the commitment of one person to another, as in the ending of *The Moviegoer* and of *The Last Gentleman*—our "handing one another along," be it Binx (who is to become a doctor) and Kate, or Will Barrett telling Dr. Vaught that he needs him. In both novels, the elusiveness and evasiveness of an egoism that protects from the risks of connection, of human relatedness, with all its responsibilities and possibilities, yield to a bond affirmed—and by the time that has happened, we readers have learned well the obstacles overcome, the apprehensions and worries that exclude us so often, so conclusively, from one another.

In his other novels, Dr. Percy pursues a not dissimilar direction, if through different pathways. *Love in the Ruins* is his sharpest, most sardonic (and gloomy) take on the end-of-the-millennium social (and moral and spiritual) situation in this country and its brother or sister nations of Europe (the so-called advanced capitalist societies). The novel also happens to be a doctor's story in the sense that Percy fills it with plenty of neuroanatomical references, drawing on his memories of medical language and medical meetings. He also alludes to the messianic aspirations of scientists, often overlooked by those ready to be skeptical of religious thinkers, but all too uncritical of what is offered in the name of the natural sciences, or even the social sciences, no matter their murkiness or pretentiousness. In *Lancelot,* a novelist who has worked in clinics and hospitals struggles mightily, ingeniously, with the heart of medicine—how one person communicates with another. "What I know, I know first from you," I once heard Dr. Williams tell a patient who wasn't as forthcoming as the good doctor wanted—needed—him to be; hence the coaxing, but also the flat-out acknowledgment that when we speak (as we so often do) of the "doctor-patient relationship," we are addressing the very matters that haunted Dr. Percy for decades, namely, as he put it in one essay, "The Mystery of Language," our distinctive human attribute. *The Second Coming* takes us back to Will Barrett, that "last gentleman"; and in the story, a writing doctor once again struggles with the vicissitudes of human connectedness—with our yearnings for and fear of others, with the loneliness Kierkegaard knew to probe intellectually, even as he experienced it in no small measure. Finally, *The Thanatos Syndrome,* by its very title, signals a doctor's inquiry into a matter that has only grown more serious and challenging in the decade or so since that (prophetic) book appeared: our secular inclination to play God with life, or, put differently, to be all too sure of ourselves as to who ought to live and why.

Then there are the essays—those two wonderfully and suggestively named books, *The Message in the Bottle* and *Lost in the Cosmos: The Last Self-Help*

Book. The first offers an ever so powerful reminder of who we are as human beings, and how we might better know ourselves, learn and remember what matters around us. When the dean of Harvard Medical School, Dr. Daniel Tosteson, was contemplating a "new pathway," a curriculum that would emphasize ideas, a manner of thinking about things, rather than the heavily rote knowledge of an accumulated factuality (tested and tested by multiple-choice questions), he went to see Dr. Percy in Covington—a significant journey, indeed. Many of the essays in that book would serve both medical students and their teachers well—and do so, in some schools. As for *Lost in the Cosmos,* it is brilliantly, humorously telling in its scrutiny of us, who are more vulnerable and sadly desperate (hence gullible) than we dare comprehend, let alone say out loud to others. True, the book is parodic, its focus social and cultural, rather than clinical; but again, a physician sees through so much nonsense, mocks so many pieties, out of a tough, medical awareness that has enabled him to be properly skeptical where others rush to embrace with unstinting enthusiasm.

In Covington and in New Orleans, all who knew Walker Percy called him Dr. Percy, even as he thought of himself in that way. Once, the two of us were wondering about our eccentric ways as graduates of Physicians and Surgeons who had strayed considerable distances from the proverbial beaten path—whereupon he said to me, hoisting a glass of bourbon (which he knew how to enjoy, to drink both stylishly and sensibly): "Once a doctor, always a doctor." I wasn't so sure, with respect to myself at least, and maybe, with respect to him as well—and I said so. Right away he rallied to his chosen profession, told me how much he thought I owed it, how much he'd learned preparing for it, how much it shaped both the way he thinks and what he had written in his essays and novels. As I wrote the words for this essay, I kept remembering that moment. His was, indeed, a doctor's mind, and back then it was watching both of us ever so sharply, writing us up, as it were: taking stock of our complaints, our symptoms, our situation, and contemplating for all of them certain remedies.

The Act of Seeing with One's Own Eyes

Ross McElwee

In 1976, while still a graduate student in film school, I shot a documentary called *Backyard*. The film begins with my telling a story over a series of photographs of my father and me:

> When I was eighteen, I left my home in North Carolina to go to college in New England, and I ended up living in Boston. Ever since then, my father, who was born and raised in North Carolina, and I have disagreed about nearly everything.
>
> When I graduated from college, my father, who's a conservative Republican, asked me what I planned to do with my life. I told him I was interested in filmmaking, but there were also some other alternatives, such as black voter registration in the South, or getting involved in the peace movement, or entering a Theravadin Buddhist monastery.
>
> My father thought this over for a moment and then said, "Son, I think your concept of career planning leaves something to be desired. But I've decided not to worry about you anymore. I've resigned myself to your fate."
>
> I didn't exactly know how to respond to this, but finally I said, "Well, Dad, I guess I have no choice but to accept your resignation."

That anecdotal preface about "resignation" sets the stage for the rest of the film, a film in which hardly anything happens—at least in terms of conventional narrative. I was interested in making a film that would be quite different from what most people think of as a documentary. I wanted it to be a highly subjective autobiographical work that nonetheless used the time-honored technique of cinema verité: no interviews, no "setting up" of scenes, no directing of people who appeared in the film. I would simply observe with my camera life as it unfolded around my father's house or in the backyard over a summer. What I was interested in rendering somehow were the unseen force fields that I felt converging and reverberating around my house and family whenever I came home. I filmed patiently over a period of two months the minutiae of daily life around the house: my physician father brushing his teeth before heading off for his morning hospital rounds; Melvin, the yardman, methodically cutting the grass; Lucille, the housekeeper, washing dishes; my brother reading a newspaper. The force fields that I hoped somehow to capture on film had to do with several things: the recent death of my mother at home after a long bout with breast cancer, my surgeon father's pride in my brother as he was preparing to depart for his first year of medical school, and finally the relationship between my family members and several black people who had worked around the house for many years. The only real narrative "event" of the film occurs when my father gives a going-away party for my brother. The next day my brother gets in his car and drives off to Tulane to begin medical school. That's it. There are no dynamic confrontations, no dramatic turn of events, no aggressively incisive interviews. Life just goes on, calmly and methodically, around the house, with me filming as much of it as I can.

I returned to Boston not quite knowing what to do with this decidedly undramatic material—some seven hours of it. What had I been after with my camera? Were these force fields—the one created by the absence of my mother, the one activated by my own filmmaking presence in the medical world of my father and brother, the one that had to do with black folks patiently cleaning up after white folks—would these psychological pressure points be detectable to a viewer? This was the question that bedeviled me upon my return to Boston after my summer of filming. And indeed I shelved the *Backyard* footage and worked instead on another film while finishing my last semester of film school. My plan was to edit *Backyard* after I graduated, when I had more perspective on the project.

Nova

I graduated from film school. But instead of getting right to work on editing *Backyard,* I found that I felt deep ambivalence and confusion about my chosen field of endeavor, documentary filmmaking. My grandfather, father, brother, and assorted relatives had all chosen medicine as a career. Why was I drawn to the arts? I was still nagged by the ideal of medicine as a life pursuit. It seemed in some ways to be the noblest of professions, coupling compassion and science, exacting the talents of the brain, the hand, and the heart, while delivering financial security in the bargain. And yet there was something about medicine that could not satisfy the strange inchoate urging I felt to render and reorder the world through the lens of a movie camera. My father would occasionally remind me that at my age—twenty-nine—he had finished his residency, gotten married, fathered three children, bought a house, and settled down to practice medicine forty miles from the small town where he had been born. He, being a surgeon, was incisive—a man who knew his place in the world. His reminders to me were meant as concerned proddings, and they succeeded in making me feel somewhat unsettled. I had to admit I could see from his point of view that I was in trouble. There I was, living in a $200-a-month studio apartment in Cambridge, Massachusetts, facing a career of freelancing in a field that was far from secure, without even a girlfriend, much less a wife.

And then there was the problem of my southern perspective. Why was I choosing to live in a dangerous, dirty, noisy, metropolitan area rendered un-inhabitable six months out of each year by subarctic climatic conditions? Why did I want to live in a city that seemed to have an unwritten ordinance against smiling at someone you pass on the sidewalk or saying hello to some-one standing in line in front of you? In fact, why live in a city that requires so *much* standing in line, or, if you're foolish enough to drive, where people use their cars as weapons? Racial tension? It actually seemed much worse in Boston than I remembered it being down south. And to reap all of these northern urban benefits, I was, in my penurious state, voluntarily opting for Boston's high cost of living—a level that was reputedly second only to Honolulu's. Was I crazy? My professional confusion at the time only served to magnify all of these perceived defects in northern living, with the result that I felt acutely out of place in Boston—ever an outsider.

Mired in this confusion, too overcome by inertia to consider moving, and confronted with a rapidly depleting bank account, I began applying for film-editing jobs around town. I was finally hired by WGBH, Boston's PBS affili-ate, to synchronize 16-mm film footage with sound tracks, the tedium of which was matched only by the precision that was required to do the job correctly. My fellow synchronizers and I worked in a warren of claustropho-bic, windowless, white-walled editing rooms for eight to twelve hours a day. When I left WGBH at night, I'd find myself unconsciously checking the world around me—watching and listening carefully to the slamming of a car door or a mother calling her children—to be certain that sound and image were in true sync.

But worse than the tedium of sound synchronizing was that, as luck would have it, the series I was hired to work on was none other than *Nova,* the PBS science series. And so, day after day, I aligned sound with image so that an endless stream of brilliant scientists, most of them, at least as I remember it, being people in various medical fields, might expostulate on assorted mysteries of the universe that they themselves were unraveling. These men and women, an inordinately high percentage of whom seemed to have the phrase "Nobel laureate" appended to their names, intoned their wisdom in carefully chosen words that even a typical television viewer such as myself could comprehend. Depressingly, they seemed to me like deities.

Lennart Nilsson in particular irked me. The noted Swedish medical researcher was one of the first to use fiber optics in his work and, even more impressively, had perfected a way of using these fiber-optic viewing systems to photograph an embryo still in the womb, as well as assorted aneurysms and other physiological catastrophes. *Nova*, of course, jumped right on this one. What could be a better marriage of film and science, after all, than being able to televise the miracle of life actually unfolding inside the human body? In fact, the program was entitled "Miracle of Life," and it was so popular among PBS viewers that WGBH used it as an enticement to garner more dues-paying members from the public. "Become a WGBH member and receive the 'Miracle of Life' for only $60.00," urged the fund-raisers, in what reminded me of the southern television preachers from my youth, selling salvation over the airwaves.

I struck back in puerile ways, excising words from audio outtakes to create a pseudo-sync sound track that had the distinguished Dr. Nilsson confessing to his interviewer, "Actually, I don't know what I'm talking about." My fellow synchers loved this, but the solace of this triumph was short-lived. For the most part, I was forced to give voice to my Nobel laureates so that they could expound knowledgeably and eloquently day after day, week after week, all of them reminding me in one way or another of my father. Was I doomed to work my way slowly up the *Nova* ladder from synchronizer to assistant editor to editor and finally producer of these talking-head science documentaries? What did I think I was going to accomplish with the strange footage I had filmed in North Carolina, footage in which the "heads," instead of talking, remained mostly silent? Had I not been trying to document on film what was essentially unseeable? Was it too late to apply to medical school?

A Book of Revelation

Then, at the suggestion of a friend, I picked up *The Last Gentleman*. I could not put it down. How was it that Percy happened to have known enough about me to have written my psychological biography? This was more than just a case of identifying with the main character. I felt that Percy had some-how gained access to my beleaguered twenty-nine-year-old soul. All the struggles I was going through were laid out for me right there in the first few pages as Percy described the troubles besetting his young protagonist, William Barrett:

> To be specific, he had a nervous condition and suffered spells of amne-sia and even between times did not quite know what was what. Much of the time he was like a man who has just crawled out of a bombed building. Everything looked strange. Such a predicament, however, is not altogether a bad thing. Like the sole survivor of a bombed building, he had no secondhand opinions and he could see things afresh.

I was grateful to Percy for both describing a condition, a way of reacting to the world, that seemed all too familiar to me, and at the same time acknowl-edging that this stance could have at least some attributes. There were other paragraphs in those opening pages that my biographer, Dr. Percy, wrote that seemed to convey to me, if not exactly personal encouragement, at least a good-humored condolence for what I was going through:

> [Barrett] did not know what to think. So he became a watcher and a lis-tener and a wanderer. He could not get enough of watching. . . . Like many young men of the South, he became overly subtle and had trouble ruling out the possible. They are not like an immigrant's son in Pas-saic who decides to become a dentist and that is that. Southerners have trouble ruling out the possible.

I could identify with Will Barrett's inability to rule out the possible as well as his tendency to "watch" the world. His "nervous condition" was familiar to me, though I cannot claim my confusion was as debilitating as were his fugue states, in which he would be in New Jersey one afternoon only to wake up in some southern Civil War battleground a few days later, having no idea how he got there. (Percy sometimes refers to Barrett, the Princeton dropout who has forsaken his studies in engineering, as "the engineer," an ironic ap-pellation to be sure, since Barrett seems incapable of engineering his present, much less his future.) More compelling to me than the amnesiac states of the young protagonist were his observations on the act of seeing. One day, Barrett makes a reluctant return to the Metropolitan Museum of Art:

> Today the paintings were there, yes, in the usual way of being there but worse off than ever. It was all but impossible to see them, even when one used all the tricks. . . . There is the painting which has been bought at

great expense and exhibited in the museum so that millions can see it. What is wrong with that? Something, said the engineer, shivering and sweating behind a pillar. For the paintings were encrusted with a public secretion. The harder one looked, the more invisible the paintings became.

Percy then describes how a workman, repairing a skylight above the gallery in which Barrett is standing, suddenly topples from his ladder with a frightening crash. In the ensuing confusion, Barrett, who has knelt by the workman's side, has an epiphany of sorts:

> It was at this moment that the engineer happened to look under his arm and catch sight of the Velazquez. It was glowing like a jewel! The painter might have just stepped out of his studio and the engineer, passing in the street, had stopped to look through the open door. The painting could be seen.

As a fledgling filmmaker, I found that passages such as these sang out to me about the problems and possibilities of seeing the world with a fresh, "unencrusted" vision.

A Telescope: Penetrating to the Heart of Things

Much of *The Last Gentleman* is about possibilities of how to view the world, to view life, and of how to make sense of the data one gathers from what appears to be a metaphysically senseless world. It is about the struggles of a young man with scientific training trying to find answers to perplexing questions that science is not equipped to answer.

Young Barrett decides that he cannot passively wait for calamitous events, such as workmen falling from ladders in museums, to catch a true vision of life under the crook of his arm. Perhaps a telescope will assist him in this endeavor. Impulsively, he purchases a telescope for $1900.00, wiping out his bank account in the process. He then sets it up next to a window in his apartment:

> He focused on a building clear across the park and beyond Fifth Avenue. There sprang into view a disk of brickwork perhaps eight feet in diameter. . . . It was better than he had hoped. Not only were the bricks seen as if they were ten feet away; they were better than that. It was better than having the bricks there before him. They gained in value. Every grain and crack and excrescence became available. Beyond any

doubt, he said to himself, this proves that bricks, as well as other things, are not as accessible as they used to be. Special measures were needed to recover them.

The telescope recovered them.

A mediating device, the telescope, brings the world, or at least a patch of brick, into the realm of the real for Barrett. It both separates him from reality and brings him closer to it. The telescope overcomes distance and achieves a different kind of closeness, a closeness sheathed in distance. He is thrilled by what the telescope recovers for him.

> It must be admitted that although he prided himself on his scientific outlook and set great store by precision instruments like microscopes and chemical balances, he couldn't help attributing magical properties to the telescope. . . . These lenses did not transmit light merely. They penetrated to the heart of things.

With his telescope, Will Barrett is, at least momentarily, able to achieve a different perspective, a different vantage point for viewing the world. He is temporarily drawn out of his suffocating existential stupor by the telescope, which confers a startling clarity on the world for our troubled protagonist. It is akin to the clarity that I, and I suspect many documentary filmmakers, have experienced upon viewing the ordinary and the mundane—the stuff of real life—through a camera lens. In that early graduate school film, *Backyard,* I felt that the methodical, even monotonous events of life around my family's house were somehow transformed when I saw them through the lens, and that the transformation was even more intense when those images were later seen projected as unedited footage. To me it seemed that the camera could have that power Percy spoke of—the "power to penetrate to the heart of things."[1]

For Will Barrett, the "magical properties" of the telescope are not unlike the magic conferred upon viewers watching a movie. The film theorist F. E. Sparshott describes how in films, as in dreams, we see from where we are not. This odd sense of displacement is familiar to all moviegoers: the sense that although on one level you realize you are watching a cinematic reconstruction of a version of the world—an elaborate optical illusion—still, that world can seem very vivid, very real. The paradox is that while watching a film, you can be psychologically and emotionally involved while being at the same time physically detached from the world you are viewing. . . . It's this odd sense of displacement, this strange detached proximity, that is akin to what Barrett experiences as he looks through his telescope.

Philosopher Stanley Cavell, who has written extensively about film, says, in *The World Viewed,* "In viewing films, the sense of invisibility is an expression of modern privacy or anonymity. . . . The explanation is not so much that the world is passing us by, as that we are displaced from our natural habitation within it, placed at a distance from it. The screen overcomes our fixed distance: it makes displacement appear as our natural condition."[2]

William Barrett seems to embody the idea of displacement as a natural condition. But he is smart enough to question this displacement, to wonder if there is any way around it, more in the direction of finding "the heart of things." The telescope has demonstrated that it can deliver a startling clarity. But what to do with this clarity? He cannot simply stare at bricks. So he takes his telescope to Central Park and begins looking at people. He watches a woman sitting on a bench. "His heart gave a leap. He fell in love, at first sight and at a distance of two thousand feet. . . . It was not so much her good looks . . . as a certain bemused and dry-eyed expression in which he seemed to recognize—himself! . . . She was his better half. It would be possible to sit on a bench and eat a peanut-butter sandwich with her and say not a word."

Percy's ironic description of his protagonist's reaction immediately subverts the possibility that this novel might become a simple love story. It could be said that Percy the author has the same detached perspective on Will Barrett that Will Barrett has on the world. And to me, at the time a somewhat confused would-be, might-be, documentary filmmaker, the tone of the novel seemed just right.

The telescope becomes for Barrett a way of trying to relate and connect to the external world, of possibly finding a passageway to an inner world, an inner life. And in fact, the woman Barrett spots through the telescope will eventually draw him haltingly out of his paralysis and back down south on an epic existential journey. At the end of the journey, and the book, it is not at all clear that Barrett has changed in the slightest. Percy is much too cagey to allow for any dramatic life changes to occur in this book. But the telescope has drawn Barrett out on a journey, a search. The idea of a search is important. Binx Bolling, another existential knight with a seat at Percy's round table, says in *The Moviegoer:* "The search is what anyone would undertake if he were not sunk in the everydayness of his own life. . . . to be aware of the possibility of the search is to be on to something. Not to be on to something is to be in despair."

Back to Backyard

Barrett employs a telescope, but perhaps if the novel had been written in 1996 instead of 1966, he might have been trying to figure out the world with a video camera on his shoulder (or at least on a tripod, for Barrett does like to keep his distance). Walker Percy himself might well have been a great practitioner of cinema verité—like Richard Leacock or Frederick Wiseman—if he had not chosen to take up writing. Upon that first reading of *The Last Gentleman,* it seemed to me that Percy had so many of the requisite skills for making interesting nonfiction films: detachment, remarkable acuity, an incisive sense of humor, and an eye for minute detail coupled with an ability to see the big picture. Percy's perspective was abetted by the fact that he was a southerner, and therefore automatically entitled to a certain degree of displacement, of being an outsider. Percy describes Will Barrett's response to returning home: "The old itch for omniscience came upon him—lost as he was in his own potentiality, having come home to the South only to discover that not even his own homelessness was at home here."

Much of the filming I had done for *Backyard* that summer explored my perceived status of being an outsider even though I had come home to the South. One of the people I filmed was Lucille Stafford, the black housekeeper who had worked part-time for my family for many years but had now really stepped in to help my father after my mother died. Because Lucille and I had known each other for so long, it was both very easy and very difficult to film her. In many ways, she seemed a member of the family, but of course, she wasn't. She was black, I was white; she was poor and without formal education, I was from an upper-middle-class background; she had had a very hard life, I had had a comparatively easy one. And of course, this was the South, where racial issues, though no less thorny than in the North, had a very different history. Lucille's grandparents had been slaves. And here she was, cooking in our kitchen. She and I had an amiable and, at times, even close relationship. But because of the complexity of race and class and southern history, it was hard to know exactly how to go about filming our relationship. In *The Last Gentleman,* I kept finding passages that brilliantly described exactly the feelings I had had when I was filming Lucille:

> Here came this strange young man [Barrett] who transmitted no signal at all but who rather, like them [the black house servants], was all ears and eyes and antennae. He actually looked at them. A Southerner looks at a Negro twice: once when he is a child and sees his nurse for the first time;

second, when he is dying and there is a Negro with him to change his bedclothes. But he does not look at him for the sixty years in between.

But Barrett is, of course, a different kind of southerner: "He was like a white child who does not grow up or rather who grows up in the kitchen. He liked to sit in the pantry and watch them and talk to them, but they, the Negroes, didn't know what to do with him."

In the footage I had shot for *Backyard* was a scene that could be described in almost exactly the same way. I am simply sitting in the pantry of my father's house, chatting occasionally with Lucille but mainly just filming the low-key kitchen activities. She asks me if I'd like some soup, which I politely decline. My brother walks in with some friends, cracks a good-natured joke, Lucille chuckles, and my brother walks out. I continue to hold the shot as Lucille continues to sit there waiting for water on the stove to boil. The shot is two minutes long—very long for a single shot in a documentary, but I very much wanted to keep it that length, without making any edits in it. How would a viewer respond to this shot if I kept it that long? Could a viewer feel what I was feeling as I filmed in that room, a feeling Percy had so wonderfully articulated with the written word? Or would I merely be subjecting a viewer to an excruciatingly literal instance of a watched pot never coming to boil? In fact, 'were people not too conditioned to potboilers to have the patience to sit through a film like the one I was thinking of making?

But for me there was something deeply evocative about this scene: the glaring noon light coming through the kitchen windows, Lucille's patience with my filming and with my brother's joking, her tired good humor, the sudden sense of absence when my brother leaves the room, the nearly mournful stillness of the kitchen with its immaculately clean white counters, the somnolent hum of the refrigerator. All these things I had sensed as I was filming and found even more vivid when I viewed the rushes. And for me, those feelings were confirmed by what Percy had written. I hadn't known it at the time, but in collecting this and other footage for *Backyard,* I had stumbled onto the prototypical ground zero of a Walker Percy test site, the southern kitchen as private proving ground where abounded the trace elements Percy himself was so interested in sampling, measuring, and quantifying with his precise prose. I had found my own epicenter from which emitted the "noxious particles" that beset Will Barrett. I swore to myself, with youthful determination, that I would not cut the kitchen shot shorter than its full two minutes.

After the untimely deaths of both his parents, Walker Percy came of age in his uncle's house in Greenville, Mississippi, with a house full of vividly recalled black servants. They populate *The Last Gentleman,* not as main characters, but as secondary figures who gently haunt Will Barrett, forcing him to confront the ironies of his own life. And Barrett's reaction was very similar to mine. Lucille's presence in my home made me question many things about my own life—questions of race and class, of course, but more: fate, absence, presence, the randomness of who gets to go and who gets to stay, the question of despair as a dominant response to life, especially with regard to the recent death of my mother. The next scene in the finished film shows Lucille picking through a box containing dozens of pairs of shoes that had belonged to my mother. My father has given Lucille these shoes to take home. Lucille and I don't talk as I film. But there is a subtle and poignant awkwardness that occurs because I, and not some camera crew, am filming her. Those are *my* mother's shoes.

What I was finding in this early experimentation with my own approaches to a highly subjective, speculative tone in my documentary work was that the experience of filming both gave me a detached perspective on what I was filming and simultaneously led me to see deeply into the world I was filming. But was this detachment a good thing?

Clinical Detachment

If I was finding certain parallels between what Percy the writer had accomplished and what I hoped to accomplish someday in my own film work, I also wondered at times about possible parallels between surgery and my particular brand of documentary filmmaking. Superficially, perhaps, there were certain things the two professions shared. Is not the moment when the surgeon prepares to slice through the flesh of the patient with a scalpel akin to the moment when the filmmaker prepares to press the button and begin shooting, with the hope of penetrating into the soul of the subject? Do the two professions not share the requirements of a steady hand, a sharp eye, meticulous attention to tools of the trade, awareness of technical detail, and a fair amount of physical stamina? And in more conventional forms of documentary filmmaking, where the film is shot with a crew of five or six people, is teamwork not as necessary as in the operating room? Perhaps these parallels are valid, but overall the two professions probably have more dissimilarities than similarities.

However, detached perspective—that necessary distancing—this seemed very much to the point when thinking comparatively about surgery and my incipient filmmaking. You have to be somewhat emotionally detached as a surgeon to be competent. But how detached did I need to be in making these films? When does the detachment become a liability? Could it not limit your sense of humanity? At some point does detachment block your ability to feel compassion for your film subjects, or, for that matter, your patients?

My father often seemed to have an attitude of benevolent detachment from his patients. At times he expressed an amusement at the sometimes hapless lives of some of these people. In fact, I heard him tell some of the exact same stories Walker Percy told to his biographer—stories of patients who when trying to master the medical terminology of their conditions would end up mangling that terminology. Fibroids in the uterus became "fireballs in the Eucharist," cardiac arrest "Cadillac arrest," and so on. (I now gather that these stories are part of the permanent medical anecdotal canon, passed from one generation to the next.) Like Percy, my father sometimes seemed to hold a dim view of humanity's chance for social, if not religious, redemption. He voted Republican and thought my liberal espousals were youthful posturing, as, in fact, they sometimes were. And yet after he died, I was told that back in the 1950s he was the first physician in Charlotte to de-segregate the waiting room of his office. He had never told me this, perhaps lest it feed my youthful liberalism.

Another anecdote I recall from my father's practice is that he became ex-tremely interested in perfecting a gastric-bypass procedure that would enable morbidly obese patients to lose significant amounts of weight and thereby resume leading a "normal" life. He was a general surgeon, and though he continued to offer the appetizers and entrées that make up the general sur-geon's standard menu—removal of gallbladders, hernia repairs, suturing of lacerations, tumor removals, appendectomies—the gastric bypass became his pièce de résistance. I wondered exactly why my father had chosen this particular procedure to research and perfect. The gastric bypass was certainly not a medically "glamorous" procedure—the kind that would land you on the cover of *Life* magazine, as had been true for the heart transplant pioneer Christian Barnard. My father's cases wouldn't even get you a sound bite on *Nova*.

But my father was a very pragmatic man, and when I asked why this had recently become the focus of his research and practice, he told me that aside from his inherent interest in the area, there were also good reasons to perfect this surgical technique from a medical marketing point of view. Al-though the initial procedures were performed only on the morbidly obese— people whose lives were actually endangered by their condition—the tech-nique might someday be in demand for people who were merely grossly

overweight, and this of course would be good business for my father's clinic.
I thought this explanation to be a little cold and calculating, but I accepted
it at face value. My father was not one to romanticize or sentimentalize his
profession.

I was, however, still curious about this work of his, and when I arranged
to attended a conference where my father delivered a paper on his research,
accompanied by "before and after" slides of his obesity patients, I did get a
somewhat different perspective. The last slide of the evening was of a woe-
fully overweight fellow (nearly 450 pounds) who was barely recognizable as
a human being. The slide was also somewhat overexposed, rendering the
poor subject all the more monstrous in his unbelievable heft. The overly
bright slide endowed the poor patient with a kind of fatty chiaroscuro and
made it seem as if even the camera had been unable to contain him in its
framing device. But instead of switching to the slide that would reveal how
much weight this person had shed, my father gestured to the front row of
the meeting room, and the patient himself proudly, though somewhat shyly,
took the stage next to my father, and in front of the slide of his former piti-
able self. I recall how my father lightly rested his hand on the man's shoulder
as the assembled physicians applauded politely. There was in that gesture,
and in my father's countenance, a sense of personal satisfaction, to be sure,
but I also detected in that placing of the hand on the shoulder a somewhat
detached but very real compassion for his patient. Perhaps I'm just romanti-
cizing this memory? No. With due respect to my stoic father, I think not. My
father's patient, a freak of nature and a member of a minority that had no
spokesman, had found a champion in my father. It was clear that the patient
himself had been given a new life to live.

I believe that my father displayed in his profession an underlying compassion for his patients, and for humanity, that he refused to wear on his
sleeve—a professional survival technique, I'm sure. As a documentary filmmaker, I've usually felt, when relevant, compassion for the people I'm filming, but I've also appropriated that detached stance from my father. Or perhaps it's just part of my genetic makeup. But I recognize it when I see it in
others. I saw the compassion beneath the surface in my father. I also sensed
it in the writing of the physician turned writer, Walker Percy. But I had to dig
a little deeper to find it in Percy. His compassion was a little harder for me to
read because his writing displayed such acerbic irony and detachment. Ap-
parently that detachment was there almost from the beginning of his life.

In *Pilgrim in the Ruins,* we read about how Percy's high-school classmates
remember him in Greenville, Mississippi: "By far, Walker's favorite activity

was observing others, as almost everybody who has known him at any point in his life attests. . . . Quiet, self-conscious, he was always on the fringe, following what others were saying or doing. . . . His friends thought Percy a shrewd judge of character. . . . But . . . What was going on in his head, they wondered, and why didn't he say more?"[3]

In *The Last Gentleman,* one might deduce that we find out what was "going on in his head" by reading about what was going on in the head of Will Barrett. The difference between Barrett and Percy, of course, is that Barrett doesn't know what to do with the odd perspective he possesses—"in the world, yet not of the world"—a perspective that allows him to observe what is happening in that world with remarkable acuity. Percy makes that curse a gift by using it to inform his writing.

But before he found writing, he was headed for trouble. In his third year of medical school, he sought treatment from a psychiatrist to deal with the depression that sometimes overwhelmed him. He felt determined not to succumb to the suicidal fate that had befallen both his father and his grandfather. And Percy began to have his own doubts about his choice of professions. It could be said that he was rescued not only by psychotherapy but by discovering the study of pathology.

Toward the end of his last year in medical school at Columbia, Percy found himself more and more fascinated by the specialty of pathology, which he described, according to Tolson, as being where "medicine came closest to being the science it should be and farthest from the arts and crafts of the bedside manner. Under the microscope, in the test tube, in the colorimeter, one could actually see the beautiful theater of disease and even measure the effect of treatment on the disease process."[4] So here we have Percy looking through the lens again to gain a perspective that suits him, a position I could certainly relate to as a documentary filmmaker.

Percy admits that by the time he had begun his internship, he had lost the desire to practice medicine as a career. He spent more and more time in the morgue, dissecting cadavers, recalling that during one span of several months he worked on more than 125 of them. It was the cadavers who literally led Percy out of medicine, when he contracted tuberculosis from his morgue work, necessitating his taking a long leave of absence from his internship. Percy himself became the patient, and during this time he began reading. It was this reading—Dostoyevsky, Kafka, Kierkegaard—that would finally convince him that he should try writing.

Writing would provide for Percy what medicine could not: a way to undertake that "search" Binx Bolling would describe in *The Moviegoer.* It would give rein to all of Percy's observational powers, powers that he could train on his personal past in his death-haunted South, as well as into the future on the possibility of finding some sort of redemption.

In *The Last Gentleman,* we see versions of both the young Walker Percy, as Will Barrett, and the middle-aged Walker Percy, in the guise of Sutter Vaught, an ex-physician trying to divine the possibilities of what he calls "transcendence." In between these two characters is a wide spectrum of secondary and tertiary characters, black and white, rich and poor, southern and northern. Upon a first reading, it is possible to say that the one thing they all share is the brunt of the author's cynicism. It would not be inaccurate to describe Percy's voice as more than a little misanthropic. He is clearly condescending to the Ohioans with whom Barrett takes up while living in New York. Percy's disdain for the stuffy, pretentious Princetonians with whom Barrett attends college is undisguised. He is merciless in lampooning the psychiatrist Dr. Gamow. He also seems generally condescending toward black people in the pages of *The Last Gentleman,* but to be fair, no less so than to the white people whose lives he sketches out.

One of the most searingly sardonic, and humorous, of these minor portraits is that of Forney Aiken, "the pseudo-Negro" photographer who gives Barrett a ride during his journey down south. On assignment from a national magazine to photograph incidents of racism in the South, the photographer has disguised himself as a black man and has inserted a miniature camera behind his tie clip to try to capture examples of racism as they unfold before him. As depicted by Percy, the man is a fool on a fool's journey. Meant to be a satirical send-up of John Howard Griffin's famous journey through the South depicted in *Black like Me,* this brief episode displays Percy at his most cynical. It's possible that some might interpret this portrait as a condemnation of civil rights journalism of the 1960s, but I don't think so. Forney Aiken is not someone on a true search, as is Will Barrett. Forney is a fraud, a self-absorbed recovering alcoholic trying to relaunch his career by hitching his star to a hot issue—racism. For me, this brief episode targets a species of documentary that could stand to be satirized: the self-righteous "social justice" documentary, a genre of documentary film or photography that often doggedly pursues evidence to fit a preordained, and usually obvious, documentary conclusion—in this case, that racism exists in the South.

Even the important supporting characters—Mr. and Mrs. Vaught, who adopt Will Barrett, and their daughter Kitty, with whom Barrett tries to imagine himself being in love—are subjected to an authorial tone that can at best be described as cynicism tinged with affectionate detachment.

A question I was dogged by as a fledgling documentary filmmaker (and still am to some extent) is how much of this detachment one could afford to embrace when making films about real people living real lives with real emotions. Could I just settle back behind a camera and record the "beautiful theater" of life itself? Just how clinical could I allow my filmmaking to be? How could I balance this detachment with a sense of humanity or compassion?

And where, if anywhere, is there compassion or humanity in *The Last Gentleman?* Percy reserves it, in my opinion, for the several main characters whom he sees as really wrestling with life's unanswerable questions: the young Will Barrett, and the older, but no wiser, Rita, Val, and Sutter Vaught. With these characters, Percy allows compassion to temper the clinical detachment and the acerbic irony that informs most of the novel—especially with the suicidal Sutter Vaught.

An Assistant Coroner

On his journey south with the Vaught family, Will Barrett keeps hearing about Sutter Vaught, the older brother of Will's on-again, off-again love, Kitty. Sutter has forsaken his career as a brilliant Harvard-trained physician. Sutter's father explains to an intrigued Will Barrett:

> "Do you know what he does now?"
> "No sir."
> "He's assistant coroner. He makes five hundred dollars a month cutting on dead people in the daytime and chasing women all night. Why he's not even a coroner. He's an assistant."

Yes, another scientist who has shucked science, although Sutter hasn't shucked it for writing or filmmaking. He's on a somewhat desperate search for a philosophy that will explain to him why he should go on living. The word "autopsy" comes from the Greek word *autopsia,* which means literally "the act of seeing with one's own eyes." (This is also the title of an experimental film by Stan Brakhage, who filmed in excruciating detail the coroner's art.) If in *The Last Gentleman* Percy is conducting a detailed autopsy on the human condition, he wields his sharpest scalpel in carving out his portrait of Sutter Vaught. Vaught, irreverent, sardonic, occasionally hilarious in his pronouncements about the world, is, under the surface, truly suffering. He has tried once before to commit suicide. And he has intimated that he will try again. It is for Vaught, even more than for Will Barrett, that Percy has reserved his compassion.

Vaught, a searcher, a seer, is suffering because he sees too acutely how existence can be viewed as nothing but pain and futility. Cadaver after cadaver confirms this. He doesn't need a telescope. He sees it with his own eyes. In his coroner's casebook, he scribbles notes on the pathology of the corpses he is examining, and he links these cases to philosophical meditations. Vaught is self-aware enough to know that he is unlikely to find an answer to how to achieve what he calls "transcendence," and he views his own efforts with a familiar bemused ironic detachment. He is, after all, a stand-in for the latter-day Percy himself.

When I first read *The Last Gentleman,* I was not aware of its author's Catholicism. The book certainly did not seem to be a description of life as a pathology for which Catholicism was the remedy, but clearly Percy's Catholicism informs the work and lends to it a preoccupation with higher life goals. It helped Percy describe what is absent from the life of Sutter and Will. They are both living a life without faith, which is, of course, different than living a life without hope. Sutter and Will do exhibit hope—hope evident in conducting their respective "searches."

Even before meeting Sutter, Barrett recognizes him as a potential fellow traveler and becomes somewhat obsessed with him. Barrett finally gets to meet Sutter, but not before first spying on him in an adjacent room through a hole in the wall. "Sutter was sitting in the wagonwheel chair, idly brandishing an automatic pistol, aiming it here and there, laying the muzzle against his cheek." Barrett becomes agitated and walks away from his knothole, only to hear the earsplitting concussive sound of the pistol going off. Assuming that Sutter has shot himself, Barrett bursts into Sutter's room.

> The wagonwheel chair was empty. He [Barrett] went lunging about.
> "You must be Barrett."
> Sutter stood at the card table, almost behind the door, cleaning the pistol with a flannel disk soaked in gun oil.
> "Excuse me," said the reeling Engineer. "I thought I heard a noise."
> "Yes."
> "It sounded like a shot."
> "Yes."
> He waited but Sutter said no more.
> "Did the pistol go off accidentally?"
> "No. I shot him."
> "Him?" The engineer suddenly feared to turn around.
> Sutter was nodding to the wall. There hung yet another medical picture, this of The Old Arab Physician. The engineer had not seen it

because his peephole was some four inches below the frame. Moving closer, he noticed that the Arab, who was ministering to some urchins with phials and flasks, was badly shot up. Only then did it come over him that his peephole was an outlying miss in the pattern of bullet holes.

Will Barrett, here reverting to a different sort of viewing device—the peephole—narrowly misses getting his head blown off. (The films of Alfred Hitchcock jump to mind here—not so much Anthony Perkins peering through a peephole in *Psycho* as James Stewart snapping photographs in *Rear Window*, for it's the Stewart character who finds that his voyeurism bounces back at him with nearly fatal results.) One doesn't want to make too much of the metaphorical implications of Percy's darkly comic peephole episode, but it is interesting to think of this as a commentary on the tendency of our young protagonist to distance himself voyeuristically from the world around him. Here, his detached stance, from which he trains what Percy calls his "southern radar" on those around him, is turned against him with almost deadly results. Did it possibly occur to Percy, as he was writing this passage, that the first camera in history was the camera obscura, a dark room with a small hole in one wall casting an inverted image of the outside world on the opposite wall? It certainly occurred to this budding filmmaker, and I personally interpreted this passage as a symbolic caveat against too much distancing in my filmmaking.

Percy is playing with point of view in this same compact passage. Point of view, called POV in film jargon, is something filmmakers have to pay a lot of attention to, dealing as it does with camera position relative to the positioning of people, objects, and landscape contained within the frame. Through his peephole, Barrett watches from the dark confines of the closet a little movie about Sutter, who appears to be preparing to commit suicide. But Sutter's point of view reveals a very different scenario. His pistol is aimed not at himself (not this time) but at a sentimental portrait of medicine, as represented by the picture of the old Arab physician, Abou Ben Adhem, "ministering to urchins" (Percy's sardonic commentary on his own lapsed medical career).

Although this episode is one of misinterpretation on the part of Will Barrett, it does bring about the meeting of the two men. One could almost schematically diagram this moment: Will Barrett, the young version of Percy, sights through the hole to gain a picture of Sutter Vaught, the older version of Percy, who sights down his pistol right back in the direction of Will Barrett's sight lines.

Where the two sight lines intersect is, for me, where the vision of these two versions of Walker Percy intersect. There, the youthful, alert (though confused) acuity of the young Percy meets the cold nihilism of the middle-aged Percy. And there, a focus begins to be achieved: the rest of the novel stops being about Will and Kitty and begins being about Will and Sutter and their mutual inquiry into what Will calls the "locus of pure possibility."

And so it is Will and Sutter in whom Percy has, in the end, the most interest. Nearly everyone else in the novel is dismissed, perhaps affectionately, perhaps sardonically—but it is clearly the plight of Will and Sutter that Percy hopes will move the reader. It is in them that he renders his compassion. It is a compassion for two men struggling to see the world clearly and honestly and to arrive at a solution for how to live with what they have learned from their seeing, or if they cannot learn to live with this knowledge, then to find the conviction to die.

If Will Barrett represents, on some level, the youthful Percy, and Sutter Vaught the middle-aged Percy, is it fair to say that Percy has invested the most empathy in the two characters who represent himself? This observation is certainly borne out by reading Tolson's biography of Percy. If this is true, then is it fair to say that there is a strict limit on Percy's capability of expressing compassion or empathy for the rest of the human race? That is, can he perhaps feel compassion only for those who have shared his particular somewhat rarefied view of life? Is the vision of the novel limited because of this? Perhaps. But I still find myself moved by the plight of the two Percy stand-ins. One must at least state that Percy has a great deal of compassion, if not for human beings, then for the human condition.

And yet perhaps even that is an unfair assessment. The episode in which Will Barrett sees the workman fall from the skylight at the museum is, of course, interesting for what it says concerning all the problems entailed in viewing "high art," but what is also intriguing about this passage is how Percy elects to move Will, the indecisive contemplator, to the fallen man's side in an instant. "The workman was not bleeding, but he could not get his breath. As they held him, and he gazed up at them, it was as if he were telling them he could not remember how to breathe. Then he pulled himself up on the engineer's arm and air came sucking into his throat. . . . It was at this moment that the engineer happened to look under his arm and catch sight of the Velazquez. It was glowing like a jewel!"

There is no transitional sentence describing how Barrett transforms himself from an existentially paralyzed artphobe, cowering behind a column, to someone immediately rendering aid to an injured man. Barrett is simply there, in a moment of literary elision or, in film parlance, in a jump cut. We see Barrett react more than once like this in the novel—as in the fight scene in the bar in which he decks a deputy sheriff to protect people who aren't really even his friends. These instances are subtle markers of Barrett's, and hence Percy's, humanity. It is not a sentimentalized, highly dramatized humanity. But Barrett, alienated from life and to some degree from the human race, still manages when called upon to exhibit his humanity. It is Percy displaying, despite himself, a good bedside manner.

The end of *The Last Gentleman* is intentionally unresolved. Sutter drives away from the hospital where his younger brother, the terminally ill Jamie, has finally succumbed to leukemia. Will runs after the car, calling for Sutter to wait. The car stops. It's not at all clear that Sutter won't commit suicide, even if Will comes with him. And it's not at all certain that they won't both commit suicide. But the spring in Will Barrett's step as he runs up to Sutter's car ("Strength flowed like oil into his muscles and he ran with great joyous ten-foot antelope bounds") indicates that Barrett, with his acute southern radar working at high frequency, senses that he and Sutter are about to corner the issue, confront it one way or the other. Having just watched young Jamie become yet another corpse, a future cadaver, right before their eyes, they both somehow know that they've seen enough. Now they have to come to terms with what they have been seeing for so long. It's an oddly powerful yet inconclusive conclusion to the long journey of *The Last Gentleman*.

Perhaps this book is less a novel than it is the autobiographical documentary diary of Walker Percy. All fiction is to some degree autobiographical, of course, but this seems to be preternaturally true with Walker Percy and *The Last Gentleman*. The replacement of conventional plot with an episodic picaresque journey goes a long way toward "de-novelizing" the work. It is also a book of ideas, a sort of journal, in which Percy offers up plenty of cosmic generalities. But there are countless passages of vivid observational writing, such as the following description of setting out on a hunting trip with dogs in the back of the car: "They drove into the woods in an old high-finned DeSoto whose back seat had been removed to make room for the dogs. A partition of chicken wire fenced off the front seat. The dogs stuck their heads out the windows, grinning and splitting the wind, their feet scrabbling for purchase on the metal seat bed."

Passages like this, which do nothing at all to "advance the plot," seem organic and real and impart to the book the edgy feel of a meandering documentary film—the kind of film I had wanted to make. This as much as any other quality was why I was drawn to *The Last Gentleman* as a young documentary filmmaker.

A Belated Thanks to Dr. Percy

I eventually quit my job at *Nova,* but not to go to medical school. Instead I finished *Backyard.* Seeing it now, some ten films later, it seems full of flaws, but I have to say it turned out mostly the way I hoped it would. (I did relent somewhat and cut my precious kitchen scene from two minutes to a minute and a half, but I suspect waiting for the pot to boil still manages to drive a portion of the audience to distraction.) The most important thing for me about making *Backyard* was that it encouraged me to keep going in my search—my search for a particular approach to making nonfiction films, an approach that entailed the use of an authorial subjective voice, or persona, in a genre that traditionally and adamantly eschews such notions.

What *Backyard* eventually led me to was the making of *Sherman's March,* a film I somehow wish I could have shown to Walker Percy before he died. I think he would have enjoyed it. The film's somewhat preposterous subtitle is "A Meditation on the Possibility of Romantic Love in the South during an Era of Nuclear Weapons Proliferation," but that's actually not a bad description of the major themes contained in the film. In the introduction, the filmmaker describes, in somber voice-over, his recent breakup with his girlfriend and his reluctance to undertake his intended project—a documentary on the lingering effects of Sherman's devastating Civil War march through the South. The film instead becomes a record of the filmmaker's halting quest to find a new girlfriend. As he retraces Sherman's route through the Carolinas and Georgia, he meets, and to varying degrees becomes involved with, seven southern women, all of whom patiently try to go about their everyday lives while being filmed. Remaining true to his original concept, the filmmaker also tells the story of Sherman's march itself, pausing at battle sites to reflect on the proliferation of nuclear weapons facilities and survivalist encampments he encounters along the way.

Several years had passed between my first revelatory reading of *The Last Gentleman* and the first roll of film I shot for *Sherman's March.* I was certainly not consciously thinking of Walker Percy or Will Barrett as I set out to follow Sherman's path. But somewhere deep in my consciousness, I'm sure that pockets of Percy informed and advised me as I intuitively groped my way through the South, trying to make sense of what Sherman had done and trying to make sense of what I was doing with my own life.

Sherman's March was, to my surprise, quite successful at the box office. More importantly, its success enabled me to make subsequent documentary feature films, more or less on my own terms. Although I am always questioning whether or not my films are working as they should, although I agonize over whether my persona, my voice in the films, seems authentic enough, I still feel very fortunate to have found at least some kind of a voice, and hence a way of seeing the world with my own eyes. As is probably true for most filmmakers, I feel I have many mentors, but Walker Percy certainly came on the scene at the right time for me, and I will always be grateful that I read *The Last Gentleman* at the particular time that I did.

Notes

1 In *Pilgrim in the Ruins,* Jay Tolson's biography of Walker Percy, it is interesting to discover that during a summer spent in Europe between his freshman and sophomore years in college, Percy spent a considerable part of his limited travel allowance on an expensive pair of Zeiss binoculars, "an extravagance he came to regret near the end of his European wanderings." From this biographical tidbit, and others like it, such as the fact that after Percy's father committed suicide, Percy inherited his father's telescope, we can surmise that the writer himself had at least a mild fascination with viewing devices. See Jay Tolson, *Pilgrim in the Ruins: A Life of Walker Percy* (New York: Simon and Schuster, 1992), 116.

2 Stanley Cavell, *The World Viewed: Reflections on the Ontology of Film* (Cambridge, Mass.: Harvard University Press, 1979), 40–41.

3 Tolson, *Pilgrim in the Ruins,* 85.

4 Ibid., 148.

Why Doctors Make Good Protagonists

John Lantos

Doctors appear commonly in twentieth-century literature. Something about them makes them attractive protagonists. They find themselves at the center of moral tales. Medicine makes a good metaphor. Often it is not clear exactly what medicine is a metaphor for, as in Kafka's "The Country Doctor," Mann's *The Magic Mountain*, or Camus's *The Plague*. But even without precision, medicine works as a metaphor for matters of spiritual, moral, and political urgency because medicine itself has a spiritual, moral, and political urgency. Something about the enterprise grabs us, so that the work a doctor does, and the way he or she does it, is important to the way we understand some of our own personal or cultural or spiritual aspirations. We so take this metaphoric connection for granted that it is somewhat surprising to see that it was not always so.

Before the twentieth century, doctors appeared in literature as buffoons. Generally ineffectual, they would appear on the scene at times of trouble and offer little assistance. Often they would be an object of scorn or pity. In some cases, they would play a ceremonial role as a village intellectual or a learned man. Generally, the doctor was not the main character of the story.

A quintessential example appears in a quintessential nineteenth-century novel, Flaubert's *Madame Bovary*. Charles Bovary is a typical nineteenth-century doctor. Throughout medical school, he cut classes, spending the time instead going to pubs and cultivating his passion for dominoes. Once in practice, "Charles trotted across the country in rain and snow. He ate omelets at farmhouse tables, poked his arm into damp beds, let blood and caught the warm spirit of it in his face, listened to death rattles, examined basins, tucked in a great many dirty sheets."

In one sense a lowly public servant, Bovary nevertheless represented enlightened ideals. Medicine promised more than it could deliver, but the promise was important. "You'll find plenty of superstition to fight against, Monsieur Bovary," a colleague warned. "Plenty of adherence to tradition, with which your scientific efforts will come in daily collision. They still have recourse to prayer, to relics, to the parish priest, rather than come along naturally to the doctor or chemist." The physician, in Flaubert's view, struggled to embody and advertise the new biological scientific understandings of disease and suffering as preferable to religion as a basis for the organization of society.

Of course, it was mostly bluff. When Charles attempts to surgically correct a clubfoot, his operation is initially thought successful. His "outcome study" appears in the local paper, which lauds his work. "Honor those tireless souls who sacrifice their sleep to the advancement or the healing of their fellowmen. Honour, thrice honour! Can we now cry aloud that the blind shall see and the lame walk? What fanaticism once promised its elect, science now achieves for all mankind!" Again, medicine is portrayed as a response to the failings of religion.

It turns out that Bovary's patient has horrendous complications. Gangrene sets in. Eventually he needs the whole leg amputated. Bovary is disgraced, and medicine itself is shown to be worse than religion, which cannot cure clubfeet but at least leaves well enough alone. The novelist seems to view the idealism of scientific medicine as mostly hype.

Chekhov, a physician, portrays doctors in a similar way. In *Uncle Vanya,* the physician represents a vaguely progressive liberal environmentalism. He doesn't seem to work much as a doctor but instead spends his energy during long house calls trying to save Russian forests and to seduce the lovely second wife of one of his patients. Like Bovary, his medicine is secondary, but it allows him to represent liberal ideas against the traditional morality of the church. Like Charles Bovary, he is not the main figure of the drama.

By the early twentieth century, this had begun to change. Doctors begin to have not just enlightened ideas but also frightening new powers. In *The Magic Mountain,* doctors are associated with wonderful new technologies. They can see our bones, diagnose disease before we feel sick, and know and understand whether we shall live and die. The doctors, in Mann's work, are beginning to take on some of the aura that they will more fully attain in later twentieth-century literature.

Sinclair Lewis's *Arrowsmith* catches the transition between the old type of doctor and the new. Like *The Magic Mountain, Arrowsmith* portrays the new commercialism of medicine. Lewis's doctors are becoming entrepreneurs, using the allure of science to sell all sorts of nostrums and quackery. In *Arrowsmith,* we begin to see the struggle for the soul of medicine, and the contrast between the honest science that alone gives medicine its powers, and the commercialization of pseudoscience, by which doctors cash in on the unfulfilled promise of science. Lewis was the first to make doctors his main characters, and to portray their struggles as a sort of paradigm for a set of moral struggles that engage us all. How do we tell science from pseudo-science in a world where science defines truth? How do we sort and separate the promises and the pitfalls of progress? Can an old cultural icon, the doctor, be adapted to fulfill new cultural needs?

Lewis played with different answers and created all sorts of doctors for readers to evaluate and judge. Max Gottlieb, the bacteriologist, a careful basic scientist who struggled to make medicine more scientific. His colleagues said that "he was so devoted to Pure Science, to art for art's sake, that he would rather have people die by the right therapy than be cured by the wrong." The popular Lloyd Davidson, who would have been an illustrious shopkeeper, and who had the students memorize the same lists of prescriptions that he had memorized as a medical student. From him, "a future physician could learn that most important of things, the proper drugs to give a patient, particularly when you cannot discover what is the matter with him." Dr. Hesselink, an honest country doctor, "careful and afraid of nothing, however much he might lack in imagination." Gustaf Sondelius, the soldier of science, who "shouted, in high places and low, that most diseases could and must be wiped out; that tuberculosis, cancer, typhoid, the plague, and influenza were an invading army against which the world must mobilize." Martin Arrowsmith travels through the world of medicine, deciding whether to be a small-town practitioner, a public health doctor, a research scientist, or a clinical investigator. Each is presented as a moral choice, and in the end, he chooses the millenarian hope of pure research as the most virtuous.

Camus makes a different use of the medical metaphor. In *The Plague,* the doctor's struggle against disease represents humanity's struggle against despotism. And it is not the efficacy of medicine that gives it power, but the virtue of the physician. Rieux does not have the power to cure any of the plague's victims, and yet his determination to struggle on, his unfailing devotion to the moral ideals of the healing profession, is offered as an example of the struggles we all must make if society is to conquer political plagues.

Walker Percy, a physician and novelist, finds doctor imagery compelling in a number of ways. His physicians are neither scientists nor particularly virtuous. Their struggles are portrayed as struggles for faith, but not for faith in the scientific mission of medicine. Instead, they are looking for a different sort of belief. In *The Moviegoer,* Binx has given up his premedical studies because the world of science bores him. He prefers selling stocks. But in the end, for reasons that seem to reflect less idealism and more of an internal balancing act of some sort, he decides to marry and go to medical school. In other

Percy novels, the main character is often a clownlike physician, in jail or in disgrace, who is contrasted with the successful, high-powered subspecialists, surgeons, or NIH researchers. The mainstream medical enterprise, in Percy's vision, has become morally neutral or even despicable, but the physician is still a compelling figure as one who can and must make moral struggles— often against mainstream medicine and the successful physicians of his time.

In this view, the morality of medicine has become something separate from the moral struggle of the physician, and yet the physician's power is still recognized as crucial for carrying on the struggle. This reflects what philosopher Jacob Needleman writes in *The Way of the Physician:* "All that the calling of the physician has represented throughout the centuries has vanished from view. It still exists, this calling, but it has retreated into the realm of the invisible, waiting for real men and women to allow its reappearance." As a result, "the doctor of today is either riddled with tension or stuffed with complacency. But above and beyond this, he is bored. He is nervous and bored or complacent and bored."[1] Bored with the mundane aspects of illness, disease, and treatment, and thus addicted to the thrills of science and innovation, of discovering even more new and dangerous approaches to therapeutics, and adhering to a more radical utilitarianism to justify these approaches.

Percy writes of doctors, but he doesn't really write either as a doctor or as a patient. His writing is unlike the autobiographical literature of medicine, which offers insights into the inner experience of being a doctor and a patient. Neurologist Oliver Sacks wrote about his care for an injury he sustained while mountain climbing. After surgery, he developed a strange paralysis of the leg. He describes the emotional vulnerability that all patients must feel as he waits for the surgeon, who is about to make a postoperative visit:

> I ought not to demand too much of him, or over-burden him with the intensity of my distress. If he was a sensitive man, he would be instantly aware of the distress, and dispel it, with the quiet voice of authority. What I could not do for myself in a hundred years, precisely because I was entangled in my own patienthood and could not stand outside it, what seemed to me insuperably difficult, he could cut across in a single stroke, with the scalpel of detachment, insight, authority. . . . I required only the voice, the simplicity, the conviction of authority: "Yes, I understand. It happens. Don't fret. Do this. Believe me. You will soon be well."

As Sacks indicates, even patients who are doctors, and who should know better, dream magical dreams and harbor mystical fantasies about what their doctor will do for them. Sickness does strange things for the mind. Almost inevitably, the sick or suffering person invests the healer with magical powers, even when he or she knows that it is inappropriate to do so. Sacks even recalls that when he once cared for a patient with a similar condition, he had been unable to respond empathetically. He knows better than to expect his doctor to do any better, but he still hopes, he still believes. This literary imagery counters some more abstract perceptions of what the doctor-patient relationship ought to be. We can see ourselves more easily in stories, perhaps, than in moral principles, and in the end, stories may be better teachers of morality. We need to learn not just what we ought to aspire to, but how easy it is to fail to reach those aspirations.

Sacks knows that as a patient, he will accept his doctor's technical limitations more easily than he will accept his doctor's failure to connect emotionally. "If he could not, in truth, reassure me, I would want an honest acknowledgment of the fact. I would equally respect his integrity and authority if he said, 'Sacks, it's the damnedest thing—I don't know what you've got. But we'll do our best to find out.' If he showed fear, frank fear, I should respect that too. I should respect whatever he said so long as it was frank and showed respect for me, for my dignity as a man."[2]

It is a rare doctor-patient encounter in which the patient's felt needs can be met, because the patient's felt needs are generally enormous, perhaps infinite. William Carlos Williams understood this as well as any writer ever has. His stories frequently start by noting his initial fear of patients' needs. He is wary, often disdainful, of the patients who have sought his services. They are rude, they expect too much, they don't deserve his time and attention, they don't need him, he doesn't want to get involved. Williams was fascinated by the mysterious process by which some patients overcame his resistance and wriggled through his emotional defenses. It didn't happen often, perhaps, but when it did, it transformed a formal, professional transaction into a morally transformative emotional bond.

In one story, "Jean Biecke," Williams writes of a child who was brought to his hospital with malnutrition resulting from neglect. "She was such a scrawny, misshapen, worthless piece of humanity," he writes, "that I had said many times that somebody ought to chuck her in the garbage chute." But as she responds to treatment, he begins to get attached to her. His initial callousness turns into affection and loyalty. When she gets a mysterious infection, he stays up nights trying to save her, consults specialist colleagues, tries everything. To no avail. "After a month of watching her suck up her milk and thrive on it—and to see those alert blue eyes in that face—well, somehow or other I hated to see that kid go. Everybody felt rotten."

For Williams, the mystery of the doctor-patient relationship is the power of those alert eyes to make a moral claim on him. He doesn't want to care, he doesn't want a mystical or religious bond, he wants to see humanity objectively, to accept the world as the hellhole it is, in which we all, no matter how innocent or guilty, suffer and die. "We know the plane will crash, the train will be derailed. And we know why. No one cares, no one can care. We get the news and discount it, and we are quite right in doing so. It is trivial." But he also knows that even though suffering can seem trivial in the abstract, he can never ignore what he calls "the hunted news I get from some obscure patients' eyes."[3] Whatever medicine has been or should be about, it would seem that it has to include this.

Or does it? Doctors, philosophers, patients, and novelists face a new challenge today. For whereas the doctor-patient relationship may be a sacred, mystical, and economically unassessable human bond, medical science is something more concrete and pragmatic, and medical technology is something more expensive and finite. The dream of both policy wonks and corporate CEOs is that the medical enterprise as a whole ought to be a rational, scientific, and orderly endeavor that addresses defined national health needs. By this dream, we should be able to evaluate different approaches to health care in terms of the way they manage to provide universal access and quality care and to stay within budgets. To do this, we must be able to measure and compare doctors and hospitals against certain parameters, and determine whether they are doing a good job. When we do this, it is hard to measure or put a price on virtue, or on Oliver Sacks's longing for recognition, or on Williams's recognizing and responding to a patient's hunted look. These are not scientifically verifiable or econometrically enumerable entities. Insistence on their importance flies in the face of clinical epidemiology, accountability, and cost-effectiveness. Objections to this approach are generally halting, apologetic, touchy-feely. What about "clinical judgment?" What about "the doctor-patient relationship?" What about "the art of medicine?"

Well, perhaps the art of medicine must go the way of the arts of astrology and alchemy, that is, be replaced by a science that does things better. As we get better at what we do, we should be held accountable to a different standard of care. You don't need clinical judgment or a good doctor-patient relationship for a polio immunization to work. Computer algorithms may improve clinical strategies for things as mundane as the treatment of a sore throat, or as complex as the ICU management of respiratory failure. This change has less to do with reform of the system than with advances in medical science. To the extent that medicine becomes scientific, it becomes routine.

But here is the problem. Routine treatments, no matter how sophisticated or miraculous, soon become taken for granted. We're no longer amazed that we can transplant a heart or prevent polio; we're outraged that these interventions aren't equitably available to all. Americans now feel entitled to bypass surgery, liver transplants, and the survival of 800-gram babies. We can evaluate these specific interventions and, at least in theory, come up with more or less objective ways to compare one with another. Skills that are quantifiable inevitably become routinized, technical, and lose their magic. But some doctor skills are impossible to quantify. The peculiar skills of a doctor that we all seek—listening, intuition, empathy—are, inevitably, unquantifiable.

John Berger wrote a biographical account of an English country doctor named John Sassal. As a young man, Sassal is interested in technical procedures, in surgery, in action and intervention. As he gets older, he becomes more and more fascinated by his patient's lives, by the diseases that are incurable, by the way they face hardship, suffering, and death. This, along with his technical skill, makes him an extraordinary doctor, but it also makes the econometric assessment of his work impossible. Berger asks, "What is the social value of a pain eased? What is the value of a life saved? How does the cure of a serious illness compare in value with one of the better poems of a minor poet? How does making a correct but extremely difficult diagnosis compare with painting a great canvas? In our society we do not know how to acknowledge, to measure the contribution of an ordinary working doctor."[4]

We are allowed by literature (and drama and film) to see and to feel what different doctors are like, and we are given benchmarks against which to measure our own experience. These benchmarks are often tough for doctors to watch because, interestingly, even though doctors are often protagonists in these literary works, they are not characters. Their own experiences and motivations are seldom explored. Instead, they are the screens against which we as a culture project our fantasies, just as, in the clinical encounter, we are often the screens on which patients project their fantasies. This need not be interpreted psychoanalytically. The fantasies need not be emotional transferences. They may be fantasies about immortality, about conquering nature, about playing out one final human family drama. Literary explorations of the work of doctors and of the dynamics of the doctor-patient relationship help us to put a value on, to measure the contribution of, an ordinary working doctor. And the recognition that such work should never be ordinary is, perhaps, one reason why medicine is so inherently literary, and why doctors make such good protagonists.

Notes

1 Jacob Needleman, *The Way of the Physician* (Berkeley: Arcadia, 1989), 54.

2 Oliver Sacks, *A Leg to Stand On* (New York: Harper Perennial, 1984), 92.

3 William Carlos Williams, *The Doctor Stories* (New York: New Directions, 1984), 69–77.

4 John Berger, *A Fortunate Man* (New York: Vantage, 1978), 124.

From Eye to Ear in Percy's Fiction:

Changing the Paradigm for Clinical Medicine

Martha Montello

Any critical effort to understand Walker Percy's fiction requires a consideration of the significance of his medical training and lifelong interest in medicine. Whether evaluated as the work of a Catholic, a southerner, an existentialist, or a satirist, Percy's novels need to be recognized as the work of a physician who turned to writing as a method of doctoring. A self-declared "literary clinician," Percy appropriated both the form and the content of clinical medicine—its rhetorical rules, its objects of knowledge, and its goals—to write novels that are essentially pathography, the delineation of the course of a disease from its first intimations to its final crisis or resolution.[1] From *The Moviegoer* to *The Thanatos Syndrome,* the formal features of his six novels are shaped by the discourse of medicine.[2] At the same time, Percy's fiction refocuses the basic epistemology of medicine, offering a new diagnostic and therapeutic model for what ails the human spirit, not only to its author but also to the medical community and the culture at large.

The Healer's Art

Percy was a trained physician whose own experience with illness, as others in this volume note, radically shaped the way he perceived his profession. When Percy began his medical education in 1937 at Columbia's College of Physicians and Surgeons, it was one of the three premier medical schools in investigative science, heavily influenced by the German emphasis on empirical research. Like Johns Hopkins and Harvard, P&S was well known at the time for focusing its training curriculum on a program of advanced science taught by professors who were for the most part freed from clinical work to concentrate their efforts on teaching and research. During his four years there, Percy became fascinated with "the mechanism of disease . . . a very beautiful idea that disease can be explained as a response of the body to an invading organism." The beauty of the scientific method was, he said, "the first great intellectual discovery of my life." As with Binx Bolling's "vertical search" in *The Moviegoer,* the attraction of science for Percy lay in "its constant movement . . . in the direction of ordering the endless variety and seeming haphazardness of ordinary life by discovering underlying principles which as science progresses become even fewer and more rigorously and exactly formulated."[3] His medical education taught him precision in using technological instruments—the microscope, test tube, and colorimeter—to view disease processes of the human body and gave him proficiency in using the epistemology of science to solve problems.

During his medical training, however, clear signs emerged that the objective "spectator" method was somehow inadequate for Percy. To the bewilderment of his friends at P&S, he was in the habit of quietly disappearing in the afternoon, taking the subway to a downtown office where he committed himself to a rigorous course of psychoanalysis with Dr. Janet Rioch. A friend and admirer of the methods of Harry Stack Sullivan, Rioch formed a strong personal relationship with her patient that proved effective in helping him to explore his troubling legacy as the son and grandson of prominent men who had committed suicide. For years, Percy had been subject to depression, moodiness, and fears for his own future. With Rioch, he searched to find a way to keep from repeating the family pattern of self-destruction. Precise diagnosis and an effective plan for treatment, however, eluded them. Concerning what ailed him, Percy later admitted that after three years, five days a week, "Dr. Rioch and I still weren't sure."[4] Dissatisfied with Freudian analysis, Percy withdrew, his illness intact, only to fall victim to a disease of the body.

In the fall of 1941, Percy was one of twelve interns working in the pathology lab at Bellevue Hospital. While performing autopsies, often without masks and gloves, four of the interns, Percy among them, contracted tuberculosis. Some thirty years later, Percy was able to say that "TB liberated me" and call the disease "a great excuse to quit medicine."[5] But at the time, his illness must have seemed anything but fortunate. Beset by mind and now by body, this "cataclysm," as he referred at another time to his illness, was as much an existential as a physical crisis. The "same scarlet tubercule bacillus [he] used to see lying crisscrossed like Chinese characters in the sputum and lymphoid tissue of the patients at Bellevue" was no longer "out there," abstracted from his sense of himself: "Now I was one of them."[6] The X ray and weight chart defined him clinically. Now he was the object to be studied.

The result was an intellectual and existential crisis that propelled Percy into a process of radical doubt about his most basic assumptions. Under the clinical gaze, he was his disease. Within the context of scientific abstraction, Percy was later to write, man is "left a stranger to himself construed as a datum," for "not only does the existing self fail to understand itself by objective science but in so doing it falls into unauthentic existence."[7]

Two years of convalescence at the Trudeau Sanitorium at Saranac Lake isolated Percy from his work as a pathologist, and during this time, he sought out not so much an alternative to science but "a shift of ground . . . a broadening of perspective." Never faltering in his allegiance to the logic and precision of the systematic inquiry of science, he nevertheless began to explore "the huge gap in the scientific view of the world." Confined by illness, he was freed to read in areas of knowledge largely unfamiliar to him: "I began to read no longer McLeod's *Physiology* or Gay's *Bacteriology*, but the great Russian novelists, especially Dostoevsky; the modern French novelists, especially Camus; the existentialist philosophers, Jaspers (also a physician), Marcel, and Heidegger." What Percy found he has called his second great intellectual discovery: "I saw one day—maybe it was something of a breakthrough, something of a turning of a corner—that science can say so much about things, objects or people, but with its very method can only utter a statement about a single object, a glass, a frog or a dogfish—or a man—only insofar as it resembles other things of its kind."[8] Science, he realized, can explain everything except what it means to be a human being living in the world.

Percy describes his stay at Saranac not as a departure from medicine but as a time of transition, a journey or pilgrimage from one kind of diagnostic and therapeutic activity to another. Reflecting on his explorations in literature and philosophy during his "rest cure," he has remarked, "Had I not gone to Saranac, I should have practiced medicine, probably psychiatry. . . . Saranac was the critical turning point."[9] However, as his fiction and essays alike bear witness through the years, Percy never really left the profession that so captivated him. Always conceiving of himself as a physician, he never removed his listing in the *American Medical Directory*. Throughout his life, he claimed more friends who were physicians than those who were writers, and he remained attentive to developments in medicine, particularly in psychiatry. Percy consistently emphasized that he thought of writing and doctoring as essentially similar activities, that he conceived of himself while writing as "a scientist who has come to the dead end of a traditional hypothesis which no longer accounts for the data at hand."[10] In essays and interviews, he referred to his writing as "a diagnostic enterprise" that requires "a nose for pathology."[11] As a diagnostic novelist, he approached the mysterious being of his created characters in the way that a competent physician approaches the unknown in a patient. As a literary clinician, Percy envisioned his work in progress as a patient for whom a physician tries different treatments until he or she finds one that works.

Presenting the Case

Percy's readings and reflection at Saranac showed him the way writing and reading fiction could be a diagnostic tool uniquely suited to exploring aspects of his own dis-ease that had been inaccessible through the conventional methods of medicine and psychoanalysis. He began to use his fiction writing as an instrument, an alternative way of knowing.

Already skilled in medical discourse, he drew on its formal elements, its categories and techniques, to write novels that are structured as clinical tales. His six novels read as case presentations, the narrative act at the center of medical communications about patients. The physician's performative telling to a medical audience, the case presentation is the story of the process of disease in one patient. From *The Moviegoer* on, Percy's fictional case presentations arrange the events surrounding a patient-protagonist's most recent outbreak of illness to highlight the pattern of sickness. In accord with its conventional form, each of Percy's fictional cases begins with the patient-protagonist's chief complaint, rendered in his own words as he initiates a request for diagnosis and treatment. Each opening paragraph in a Percy novel is, in fact, a carefully crafted response to an unvoiced physician's traditional opening question, "What seems to be the trouble?" *The Moviegoer* is characteristic for the way it begins with a clearly agitated Binx Bolling presenting his symptoms with the words "This morning I got a note from my aunt." The novels begin in medias res, as all medical cases do, with the immediate now of the disturbance that brings the sufferer to tell his story. The clinical narratives then move through the past medical history, the social history, and the history of present illness in the traditional pattern that seeks to make sense of this most recent outbreak of illness in this one individual. The narrative progresses, though not in linear fashion, through the standard format, aiming toward a diagnosis, a plan for treatment, and a strongly implied prognosis for the suffering protagonist.

Case history, however, is always a double narrative, a medical report of an illness constructed from the patient's story. Traditionally, the patient's subjective, discursive telling is subsumed in the medical retelling and translated into a succinct biomedical account of the evidence documented by the physician. Abridged and reformed according to strict criteria for inclusion and exclusion, the patient's story is systematically purged of what are deemed subjective elements so that the physical disorders of the patient's condition will become the clear focus of attention.[12] By medical custom, the case is presented, in both its written and its spoken forms, by an effaced first-person narrator. Aiming for the appearance of a scientific objectivity interchangeable with the presentation any other physician would give under the same circumstances, the effaced narrator implicitly claims a rational scrutiny of the evidence. Nevertheless, first-person narratives are intrinsically suspect. Although the medical community characteristically chooses to ignore it, every case presentation is, to a significant degree, the teller's tale. The case historian shapes the story heard according to his or her interpretive filters. The way a physician sees and hears determines, to a large degree, what is seen, heard, and found. As every young resident is painfully aware, every case history is only as "true" as the physician's listening and interpretive capabilities permit it to be.

Reforming the Case

In turning to writing fiction, Percy found a way to explore his own dis-ease that was not accessible to the methods of either Dr. Rioch or biomedicine. Having succeeded in his objective to become a physician—perhaps intent on becoming a healer because he unconsciously needed to be healed—he nevertheless failed to find relief for his own predicament through science alone. Drawing on the cognitive rules and formal structures of medical investigation that become second nature to a trained physician, Percy found that he could alter standard clinical discourse in significant ways in his novels to gain access to what was otherwise inaccessible. As he put it, he sought "to make the unspeakable speakable."[13]

  Breaking with medical convention, his case histories return the voice to the patient. Four of the six novels are written as first-person narratives. And the two Will Barrett novels, *The Last Gentleman* and *The Second Coming,* as Lewis Lawson has convincingly asserted, seem to be written by a narrator who is viewing his younger self after years of reflection.[14] Both types of narrative voice allow Percy a way of providing a medical history through the patient's own eyes, preserving the subjective experience. The novels are akin to A. R. Luria's famous "syndrome analyses," familiar to Percy, in the way they integrate two distinct epistemological modes, the analytic and the phenomenological. Like Luria, Percy created "a picture of disease" in clini-

cal tales whose fusion constitutes both a structural method and a philosophical stance without which necessary aspects of reality would be lost.[15]
Yielding no less than a radical change in the way physicians usually think
about patient's diseases, Luria's—and Percy's—clinical histories provide a
phenomenology of illness, the portrayal of a lifeworld fragmented and transformed by sickness.

Without exception, Percy's protagonists are sick, "at various stages of disorder," as Percy put it."[16] They exist on what Susan Sontag in *Illness as Metaphor* has called "the nightside of life," each one sicker than the last.[17] All of
them, taken separately in each novel and as a composite patient of Percy's
work, are on a search for insight into their condition, a pilgrimage, a journey
from sickness to health. Typically, the Percy protagonist is a man who, by all
objective criteria, has everything he needs. Well educated, wealthy, successful with women, he nevertheless suffers from a malady he does not understand that threatens to destroy him utterly. Burdened with a secret psychic
wound, Percy's sufferer has a brooding, weak, or distant father, an alcoholic
or cuckold or bribe taker, who either tried to or did kill himself. Always,
though, there is the implication that the protagonist's predicament derives
from more than some specific chemical or physiological or psychopatho-
logical malfunction, that it is somehow inextricably linked with a larger
existential feeling of loss or despair inherent in the declining human condition. "It may be possible," Percy suggests in an early essay, "to speak of the
sickness of Western man."[18] With a physician's concern for how the patient
is doing, Percy returns to his ailing protagonists in novel after novel to adjust
the diagnosis and plan for treatment for an ever more precarious condition.
Perhaps not surprisingly, then, less than a year after the publication of *The
Thanatos Syndrome,* he suggested that his next novel might have returned to
Binx Bolling at a later stage in life.[19]

Throughout the novels, Percy depicts a broad variety of physicians who attend the ailing protagonist. Relationships between physicians and patients,
in fact, increasingly hold center stage in the novels and become the medium
through which the stories acquire their meaning. More often than not, the
physician occupies an ambiguous position in which the culturally idealized
man in white misdiagnoses the patient and somehow thwarts his progress
toward healing. *Love in the Ruins* is characteristic. The beneficent though ineffective physician (in this case, Max Gottlieb) has his dark double (Buddy
Brown), who is highly effective in achieving his unintentionally destructive
ends. In the physician-patient protagonist, Dr. Tom More, the Janus head
of the physician's self-image and social role finds disturbing form with the

rising sinister power of Art Immelmann, who may or may not be a product of Tom's own drugged imagination.

Time after time, the Percyean physician who tolerates no deviation from a strictly scientific approach fails to diagnose correctly what ails the patient and often does more harm than good. Trained only in the biomedical model of human sickness, the physician cannot see (he misses it!) the relationship between the organic process of the body and the patient's experience of it. Taking the empirically verifiable symptoms to be the illness, the physician treats symptoms in order to eradicate them, failing to comprehend why when the patient's condition deteriorates. Percy makes it clear that some human illness—and indeed some aspects of all human illness—elude the scientific approach. The physician may need another way of knowing, a different epistemology. The issue is delicately balanced in each novel: Does the physician, in wiping out the symptoms, also wipe out the patient's greatest ally, the most reliable clue to what truly ails him? Or, as the scientific community proclaims, are genetics and biochemistry, the empirically verifiable, the sole cause and determinant of who we are and of what goes wrong when we fall ill? As Will Barrett in *The Second Coming* desperately demands to know, "Does it all come down to chemistry after all?"

Models of Consciousness

From Binx Bolling on, Percy's suffering protagonists, split off from self and others, are all encouraged by the medical community and the culture they live in to privilege science. They use its visual instruments of technology to interpret their world and, alone and alienated, to try to draw it nearer. But their projects inevitably fail, for used exclusively, the scientific viewing devices so relied on—movie screen, telescope, lapsometer, video camera, imaging machine, and computer—are all depicted as insufficient and decidedly destructive. Technological instruments focused on the human subject for diagnostic and therapeutic purposes in the novels distort the user's vision and widen the painful split between the man who sees and what he sees, leaving him in worse shape than ever.

What if, Percy is asking, our model of consciousness is itself distorted? What if the lens through which we view reality distorts our perception? In each of the novels, the protagonist uses a technological instrument as an interpretive filter to apprehend and correct what ails him. In *The Moviegoer*, Binx Bolling is like one of Plato's wall watchers from "The Allegory of the Cave," granting a heightened reality to the images on the screen, a reflection of the willingness of contemporary culture to trust the reality of sense data abstracted by science over sense data directly experienced. Only larger-than-life movie stars moving across the dream screen are able to break through the deadening everydayness that characterizes Binx's world to connect authentically with themselves and others.[20] In *The Last Gentleman,* an isolated, alienated Will Barrett has fallen prey to the dominance of science with the German-made telescope through which he attempts to connect with the extended world. Unable to experience his own world directly, he significantly uses the last of his inheritance to purchase the instrument that he trusts will confirm the reality of what he sees with his own eyes: "It was as if the telescope created its own world in the brilliant theatre of its lenses."[21] Tom More of *Love in the Ruins* pins all his hopes on his invention, the lapsometer, which quantifies and objectifies everyone within its range, with comic but disastrous results. When Lance Lamar uses a defective television monitor in *Lancelot* to try to discover what plague has been visited on his house, the result is a horrific, inverted picture of reality that transforms human beings into carnal, predatory beasts. Will Barrett returns in *The Second Coming* as a now twenty-year-older suicidal lawyer. Wrongly assuming that the imaging machines of modern medicine can correctly see into what ails him, he is nearly destroyed instead by the very technology touted by his doctors for its diagnostic accuracy. And when an even more distressed Tom More returns in *The Thanatos Syndrome,* the very success of his computer in isolating the symptoms of disease tempts him to ignore the actual illness, with potentially disastrous consequences.

As visualizing devices, each of the technological instruments in Percy's novels reflects a physician's training in the standard biomedical model of disease. Modern medical technology has been highly successful at designing and using diagnostic instruments that emphasize what can be seen in the form of images, charts, and scans over what can be heard by listening to the patient. The switch has been from ear to eye. Where once diagnoses were made principally from hearing the patient's story, words are now taken to be far less reliable than "objective," empirically quantifiable evidence. Contemporary bioscience is now characterized by a hypervisualism that reduces experience to what can be proven by the eye. In accord with the primacy of sight in Western culture and epistemology, medical science identifies the presence of disease only when it can be measured and confirmed by sight. Increasingly a test orderer and a technologist, the physician relies on the X rays and scans proliferated by the imaging revolution in medicine.

The danger, though, is that thinking of disease only in terms of its anatomical expression leads the physician to think of it as an object, separate from the unique human being who is ill. In philosophical terms, the disease is reified. The forty-two-year-old man, husband and father, lying terrified in a bed in room 212 becomes "the heart in 212." The image or number that confirms the presence of disease, measured and quantified by the eye, "fixes" the disease as an object among other objects in the world. Fittingly, Percy's fictive physicians are people of the eye. From *The Last Gentleman*'s Dr. Gamow to *The Second Coming*'s Dr. Vance Battle, they look for disease rather than listen to the patient. Virtually unable to speak and hear as one human being with another, they participate in "the silent art," Virgil's description of the practice of medicine. These physicians fail to hear the story of the sufferers who come to them, have never developed the capacity for empathy that comes with learning how to use their ears as well as their eyes. The world of medicine in the novels is one of silence between patients and physicians, in which physicians are extensions of the visualizing diagnostic instruments they use, conduits for the power of the eye.[22]

Technological instruments in the novels are distancing devices, splitting the seer off from the seen as they reify everything in their visual path. Part and parcel of the wider cultural Cartesian sickness, the schizoid condition that typifies Percy's ailing protagonists distorts vision and prevents the possibility of hearing in what Percy calls "the monstrous bifurcation that sunders the self from itself."[23] Sundered men in a riven world, Percy's protagonists follow a path of progressive deterioration. Alienated and dislocated, like Sartre's twentieth-century outsiders, they have "a way of seeing things," Percy acknowledged in an interview, that "psychiatrically . . . would be considered as a pathology."[24] Their narratives portray an existence where a diagnosis of sanity rests largely on the capacity to adapt to an insane world. Through their stories, they reveal the strategies by which they live with unbearable anxiety. From Binx Bolling, king of the laid-back cool outsider, through the far more disturbed Will Barrett and the psychotic Tom More, Percy tracks the downward spiral of the malaise to the insane violence of Lancelot Lamar and an older Will Barrett, who will bear it no longer and finally points a gun at his own head. Binx's struggle to comprehend his father's self-inflicted death gives way to Will's own plans for suicide and an older but not much wiser Tom, who must at last come to terms with an entire culture's bent toward self-destruction.

Healing Fictions

In each case, the structure of medical discourse gives comprehensible shape to an examination of what ails these men whose dependence on the hyper-visualism of science divorces the outer social self from its own inner anguish. Percy's portrayals achieve a kind of double vision that keeps the difficult balance: Who's crazy here? The disturbed outsider or the menacing world around him? As the world grows more threatening in *The Moviegoer*, Kate gives words to the schizoid sense of heightened risk that runs through all the novels: "It's not any one thing, it's everything. It's all so monstrous." [25]

Only when ordeal intrudes on a Percyean protagonist does he recognize his predicament as a despairing, alienated man, split off from self and others. Percy admits that "suffering is an evil" but asserts that "at the same time through the ordeal of suffering one gets these strange benefits of lucidity, of seeing things afresh." [26] Time and again he wrote in his essays of the man who "comes to himself" when threatened with physical danger. "The Man on the Train" explains the way pain brings even the most alienated spectator back to his body, awakens consciousness to the here and now: "[The] commuter on the New York Central had a heart attack and had to be taken off at Fordham station: Upon awakening he gazed in astonishment at his own hand, turning it this way and that as though he had never seen it before." What has happened to him, Percy says, "can only be called a revelation of being . . . a theme I use in all my novels: the recovery of the real through ordeal. It is some traumatic experience . . . in each case. You have the paradox that near death you can become aware of what is real." [27]

However successfully a Percy protagonist may come through ordeal to recognize his malaise, his condition will continue to worsen until he begins to question the very way that he sees. To undergo such a radical change in consciousness, he must first discard his faulty visual instrument, his distorted way of knowing. So Binx gives up going to the movies, Will literally trashes his telescope, Tom abandons his lapsometer, Lance blows up his movie-making equipment, and the older Will makes a clean escape from the hospital with its imaging machines.

Once freed from the dominance of sight and science, each protagonist turns away from his visual instrument and toward another person with whom he begins to find a healing connection through language. For the suffering protagonist, hope lies in the words spoken between people who matter to each other. At the end of *The Moviegoer*, Binx comforts his young stepbrothers and stepsisters over Lonnie's death and talks Kate through to the courage necessary for her to find help for her depression and anxiety. In the final scene of *The Last Gentleman,* Will runs after Sutter, hoping to continue their conversation. At the end of *The Second Coming,* he learns a whole new language of authenticity with Allie in the greenhouse. In the final pages of *Lancelot,* a deeply disturbed Lance Lamar is nevertheless able to turn away from the narrow window of his cell-like room, at last willing to hear the news that Father Smith has come to tell him. In the same way, Tom More learns in *Love in the Ruins* and relearns in *The Thanatos Syndrome* the saving power of languaged love with his family.

Only in his final novel, *The Thanatos Syndrome,* does Percy provide an alternative instrument for knowing, a model of full consciousness, for his protagonist. When Father Smith offers Tom the azimuth, which means "the Way" in Arabic, he gives the suffering doctor both a diagnostic tool and a plan for treatment. The instrument that locates forest fires through the Percyean process of "triangulation" denotes the basic shape of intersubjectivity. Through such an instrument, consciousness regains its full etymological sense as a "knowing with." When a speaker and a hearer apprehend a sign in common and speak it to each other, meaning is constructed between them. The image of the azimuth is an apt one, Percy understood, for physician and patient who together connect through language and construct a meaning between them. Similar to the way of knowing that allows the writer to plumb the mysteries of his characters, the physician approaches through talk the unknown in his patient as one troubled human being with another. In such a risk-free encounter, the person heard allows himself to connect with the listener, dissolving the isolation that has characterized the existence of them both. Tom More's final conversation with a patient at the end of *The Thanatos Syndrome* illustrates just such a process under way in a clinical interview. For Percy, a healing wholeness comes through talking and listening. Always languaged, intersubjectivity is the one true and healing connector between people.

After the publication of *The Thanatos Syndrome,* Percy confirmed the way his writing had become "more diagnostic" through the years, acknowledging a growing resonance of medicine with his work. Woven through the several other discourses of philosophy, semiotics, religion, and politics that combine to form such a complex texture in the novels, the single thread of medical discourse inscribes the fiction with a scientific authority that paradoxically accounts for the success with which it challenges one of the dominant paradigms of biomedicine. Diagnostic and therapeutic, the entire enterprise of Percy's fiction was undertaken in hope, not only for himself but also for the profession he loved. Like the narrative act of case presentation, Percy's novels move from dis-ease through to health and resolution. Suggesting a microcosm of a new model for diagnostic interpretation, for a way of doing medicine, he offers a richer model of consciousness, a way of knowing to heal the sundered spirit in a troubled world.

Notes

1 Walker Percy, "The Diagnostic Novel," *Harper's Magazine*, June 1986, 40.

2 Walker Percy, *The Moviegoer* (New York: Noonday, 1967). References to the five subsequent novels are in each case to the Farrar, Straus and Giroux trade edition.

3 Walker Percy, "From Facts to Fiction," *Book Week*, 25 December 1966, 5, 9.

4 Robert Coles, *Walker Percy: An American Search* (Boston: Little, Brown, 1978), 162.

5 Carleton Cremeens, "Walker Percy: The Man and the Novelist," in *Conversations with Walker Percy*, ed. Lewis A. Lawson and Victor Kramer (Jackson: University Press of Mississippi, 1985), 34. Hereafter cited as *Conversations*.

6 Percy, "From Facts to Fiction," 9.

7 Walker Percy, "The Coming Crisis in Psychiatry," *America*, 5 January 1957, 415.

8 Percy, "From Facts to Fiction," 5.

9 Robert Taylor, *Saranac: America's Magic Mountain* (New York: Paragon, 1988), 236.

10 Percy, "From Facts to Fiction," 9.

11 Percy, "Diagnostic Novel," 40.

12 Kathryn Montgomery Hunter, *Doctors' Stories* (Princeton, N.J.: Princeton University Press, 1991).

13 Percy, "Diagnostic Novel," 41.

14 Lewis A. Lawson, *Still Following Percy* (Jackson: University Press of Mississippi, 1996), 112.

15 A. R. Luria, *The Mind of a Mnemonist*, trans. Lynn Solo Taroff (New York: Basic Books, 1968).

16 John Griffin Jones, "Walker Percy," in *Conversations*, 275.

17 Susan Sontag, *Illness as Metaphor* (New York: Vintage, 1977), 3.

18 Percy, "The Coming Crisis in Psychiatry," 415.

19 Walker Percy, from remarks made during a reading of his work, New York, Books and Company, April 1987.

20 Lewis A. Lawson, "Walker Percy's *The Moviegoer:* The Cinema as Cave," in *Following Percy* (Troy, N.Y.: Whitston, 1988).

21 Percy, *The Last Gentleman*, 5.

22 See Jay Katz, *The Silent World of Doctor and Patient* (New York: Free Press, 1984), and Howard M. Spiro, *Doctors, Patients, and Placebos* (New Haven, Conn.: Yale University Press 1986).

23 Percy, *Love in the Ruins*, 3.

24 Jones, "Walker Percy," 275.

25 Percy, *The Moviegoer,* 118.

26 Bradley R. Dewey, "Walker Percy Talks about Kierkegaard: An Annotated Interview," in *Conversations,* 121.

27 Walker Percy, "The Man on the Train," in *The Message in the Bottle* (New York: Farrar, Straus and Giroux, 1975), 88.

Prozac and the Existential Novel:

Two Therapies

Carl Elliott

In 1993 Peter Kramer published an exceptionally thoughtful book about pharmacology and the pursuit of happiness called *Listening to Prozac*. Kramer is a psychiatrist, and his aim in the book, at least in part, is to explain how the antidepressant Prozac changed the lives of some of his patients. I use the word "antidepressant," but in fact that is the controversial part of the book: the patients he describes are generally not clinically depressed.[1] They are people who just can't seem to get their lives together. Kramer writes about a doctor he calls Gail, who is very thin-skinned, who can be practically paralyzed by minor snubs or insults. She is married to another doctor; has two lovely twin daughters, perfect hair, and migraine headaches; spends more than 20 percent of her income on clothes; and to get through a typical day takes Xanax, Fiorinal, Buspar, Inderal, and Restoril. She comes to Kramer because, she says, "I'm taking too many pills for a woman who has nothing wrong with her."[2] Another patient is a forty-one-year-old bank manager who is very shy, single, and whose life is flat and monotonous and tedious. She lives at home with her parents and has only a few friends. She tells Kramer, "I don't know who I am."[3] Another patient, whom he calls Hillary, seems to suffer from a kind of terminal ennui. She's bored, lonely, uninterested, and unemployed. She can't get excited about anything and can't figure out why. She says, "The whole world seems to be in on something I just don't get."[4]

But most of these stories have happy endings. When Kramer puts these patients on Prozac, they are transformed. The shy ones become confident and outgoing; the anxious, compulsive ones become more easygoing and laid-back. Sphincter tones relax considerably. These patients say things like "This is how I've always wanted to be," and "I never really felt like myself until now." What is unusual (and controversial) about these stories is how well these people respond to an antidepressant even though they do not have major depression. They may be alienated, shy, compulsive, unhappy, lonely, or lacking in self-confidence and self-esteem, but clinically depressed they are not. Or at least not according to standard texts such as the *Diagnostic and Statistical Manual of Mental Disorders (DSM-IV)*, according to which the symptoms of depression involve things well beyond garden-variety unhappiness. If a patient is not tearful, inappropriately guilty, having trouble concentrating, losing sleep, losing weight, thinking about death or suicide—in short, if she is not clinically depressed—yet she responds to an antidepressant, then what exactly is that antidepressant treating? A personality disorder? Unhappiness? Existential dread?

Most people who need antidepressants, and who respond well to Prozac, are very different from these kinds of patients. Major depression can be lethal. Up to 15 percent of patients who have major depression commit suicide. For such people, antidepressants can be lifesaving; about 75 percent of patients who have severe major depression will respond to an antidepressant of some sort.

But the patients Kramer describes are different. Many seem to be people whose lives don't seem to have any direction, who feel empty and confused, who don't know who they are or where they are going. In fact, they sound eerily like characters from Walker Percy's novels, like Charley Parker in *Love in the Ruins,* the local golf pro who invented night golf courses but has taken to sitting at home in his Naugahyde recliner with his shorts pulled up high and saying things like, "Doc, this morning I looked at myself in the mirror and I said, Charley, who in the hell are you? What does it all mean? It was strange, Doc. What does it all mean, is the thing."

If Charley Parker's symptoms sound similar to the symptoms that Kramer describes, even more similar is the Prozac-like ontological lapsometer, a "caliper of the human soul" with which Dr. Tom More, the hero of *Love in the Ruins,* can diagnose (and eventually treat) existential illnesses. More is an ex-mental patient and psychiatrist whose patients suffer not from major depression or schizophrenia but from things such as ennui, generalized anger, or free-floating anxiety. They tend to be men such as P. T. Bledsoe, a sixty-year-old churchgoing Knothead with blinding headaches and seizures of rage who thinks he is the object of conspiracies by the Negroes, the Communists, and a Jewish organization called the Bildebergers, which he believes has taken over the Federal Reserve system. Or Ted Tennis, a well-spoken graduate student with free-floating terror and an identity crisis. He comes to More with a request for a Bayonne rayon training organ, because (as he puts it) he cannot "achieve an adequate response" with his wife. Using the ontological lapsometer, More diagnoses Tennis with "angelism," which means that he "has so abstracted himself from himself and from the world around him, seeing things as theories and himself as a shadow, that he cannot, so to speak, reenter the lovely ordinary world." Such a person, says More, is "doomed to haunt the human condition like the Flying Dutchman."

Unless, that is, he is successfully treated, which is just what Percy's lapsometer is eventually altered to do. Art Immelman, a Mephisophelian character who claims to be a government-business liaison (but looks more like the kind of man who used to service condom vendors), approaches Dr. More with an offer to fund production of the lapsometer. With a little tinkering, Immelman adjusts the lapsometer so that it becomes a tool of treatment as well as diagnosis, an instrument that can relieve existential ailments with ionizing radiation. The adjustment turns out to be both a blessing and a curse. It offers the promise, says More, of bridging the chasm between body and mind, of restoring the self to itself. Yet in the wrong hands (and there are many), it may even inflame the ills of the spirit to which human beings are prone. "If a man is already prone to anger, he'll go mad with rage. If he lives affrighted, he will quake with terror. If he's already abstracted from himself, he'll be sundered from himself and roam the world like Ishmael."

Love in the Ruins is, among other things, a satire about the idea of treating spiritual problems as medical complaints. And something similar to Percy's concerns in *Love in the Ruins* seems to hover around the objections Peter Kramer's critics have expressed about treating nondepressed patients with antidepressants. Many of them seem to think that Prozac robs people of their uniqueness or their creativity, or that it fixes a patient's outward psychological symptoms without addressing his or her underlying problems, or that patients who take Prozac become happier without ever coming to grips with the deeper causes of their unhappiness. But Kramer argues persuasively that these notions about Prozac are mistaken—that some people on Prozac do much better in therapy, that they have more capacity for insight and self-reflection, that they find themselves more creative, more energetic, more capable of enjoying life.

Yet even those of us who find Kramer persuasive often have lingering worries about the idea of treating at least some of these patients with antidepressants. What if Prozac does, in fact, treat existential ailments? What if it really does make a person feel less alienated, less fearful of death, more at home in the world, more certain about how to live a life? Is there anything wrong with this?

Percy himself had more confidence in the novel than in psychiatry as a way of dealing with these problems. As other essayists in this collection have pointed out, Percy saw his novels as a sort of clinical exercise. As he put it, the novelist needs a "nose for pathology." He sniffs the air, squints an eye, takes a hard look around and says, "Something has gone wrong here." Percy says that he and his reader stand in relation to each other as a doctor stands to his patient in the examining room: as two people, one of whom knows that something has gone wrong with the other one.[5]

That, of course, is diagnosis, not therapy, which is a rather different matter. Yet it is not too far-fetched to think of the novel also as an instrument of therapy, at least for a certain sort of spiritual ailment. Which is to say that if you are alienated and empty and lost in the world, then you may well find it therapeutic, in a very peculiar and backhanded way, to read a novel about a person who is alienated and empty and lost in the world. Created in the act of reading such a novel is what Percy calls a "community of the alienated," which, simply by virtue of what it is, serves to relieve the very alienation that the reader recognizes in himself. There is a difference, as Percy wrote in his famous essay "The Man on the Train," between a commuter on a train who feels bad without knowing why and that very same commuter reading a book about a man who feels bad without knowing why. Whereas (as Percy didn't add but might have) there is no difference between the commuter who feels bad without knowing why and the same commuter reading a copy of *DSM-IV*. Or if there is a difference, it is that the commuter reading *DSM-IV* probably feels a lot worse than he did before he started.

What I am suggesting is that a certain type of novel may be one way of making the alienated commuter feel better, or at least a little less bad. The alternative, of course, is for the commuter to get off the train and make an appointment with a psychiatrist, or even a family doctor, who could prescribe him a green-and-white pill. This is the solution for which Kramer argues, at least for some patients, and he addresses Percy's worries about it in a chapter of his book called "The Message in the Capsule." Yet I think Kramer misses (barely, but still misses) the real point of what Percy was up to.[6] Kramer suggests that Percy may well have realized the value of Prozac for the kinds of people he wrote about, and perhaps even endorsed it, if he had just realized that what he once thought were spiritual problems were, in fact, biological problems. I don't think so. I think that Percy was quite aware that many of the problems he was describing have some basis in biology, as all of mental life does. But in *Love in the Ruins* he is aiming at a more complicated idea.

Part of what Percy is satirizing with the ontological lapsometer, of course, is simply psychiatry's preoccupation with what Percy sometimes called the "objective-empirical." (At the time of *Love in the Ruins,* this would have been mainly behaviorism, but by the time of *The Thanatos Syndrome,* it would more likely be biological psychiatry.) By developing an instrument that can measure and quantify existential illnesses, Percy is making the familiar point that the mind is not the brain, and that simply because a problem can be explained in biological language does not rule out all other explanations. Just because I can explain your depression using terms such as "serotonin reuptake inhibition" doesn't mean you don't have a problem with your mother.

But Percy is also aiming at a subtler point, which is that to treat existential problems such as alienation as scientific problems is a kind of category mistake. It is a fundamental misperception of what is going on, like bumping into a lamppost at night and saying "Excuse me." This is the kind of mistake that, once you correct it, shifts you into a completely different way of seeing things. If a person is depressed by the emptiness of life as an American consumer, you are missing the point if you try to see this as a psychiatric issue. Seeing this as a psychiatric issue is like seeing holy communion as a dietary issue. It is not completely off base, but you have misunderstood something crucial about what is going on.

So what *is* going on? Part of what is going on is what Binx Bolling speaks of in one of my favorite passages in *The Moviegoer*, when he explains what he calls his "vertical search." In the vertical search, Binx has been reading books such as *The Expanding Universe*, the greatest moment of which came when he sat in a hotel room in Birmingham and read a book called *The Chemistry of Life*. Binx says, "When I finished it, it seemed to me that the main goals of my search were reached or in principle reachable, whereupon I went out and saw a movie called *It Happened One Night*, which was itself very good. A memorable night. The only difficulty was that though the universe had been disposed of, I myself was left over. There I lay in my hotel room, obliged to draw one breath and then the next."

What Percy is getting at here is that whatever the value of science might be, it is not going to say very much to a particular person about how to live a life, much less the commuter on the train who is sad and doesn't know why. And this is where Percy's insight about the novel comes in. The novel—and, for that matter, the film—by its very nature is able to do things that any sort of scientific approach to alienation cannot. A scientific approach is going to say something about alienation in general—about the characteristics that most alienated people share. Whereas the aim of the novelist, unless she is a very bad novelist, is to say something not about alienation in general but about a particular person in a particular circumstance. Not Anyone Anywhere, but Binx Bolling, a moviegoer living in Gentilly. And by talking about one particular person in a particular time and place, the novelist can, in a way, slide around the objective-empirical and take a subjective point of view—the subjective view of a particular person that we, the readers, can adopt. Because there is a sense in which Percy's reader actually sees the world through the eyes of Binx Bolling or Will Barrett or Tom More.

This is a very neat trick. Percy realizes that if you are alienated, it is often precisely because you feel as if you are Anyone Anywhere—a person for whom anyone else in relevantly similar circumstances might be exchanged, an exemplar of the general type Alienated American. And if you are Anyone Anywhere, to hear yourself described as a specimen of the type Alienated American—a type who lacks inclusivity and meaningful relationships and has not fulfilled her creative potential—well, if you have already loaded your revolver, this may be enough to make you put the barrel to your head. An alienated person who has just finished reading *The Seven Spiritual Laws of Success* is about seven steps closer to total despair. Whereas if a novelist tells you not about the type Alienated American but about Binx Bolling, a stockbroker living in Gentilly, who, now that you mention it, seems to be in very much the same predicament as you, then you may start to feel just a little less bad.

There is a scene in *The Moviegoer* where Binx and Kate go to see the movie *Panic in the Streets,* starring Richard Widmark, which is set in New Orleans; in fact, it's set in the very neighborhood where Binx and Kate see the movie. After the movie, Kate looks around the neighborhood and says, "Yes, it is certified now." It is certified because the movie has given the neighborhood a kind of legitimacy, a reality that it didn't have before. As Binx says, "if a person sees a movie which shows his very neighborhood, it becomes possible for him to live, for a time at least, as a person who is Somewhere and not Anywhere."

I think something similar goes on for the reader who sees his predicament in a novel or a movie. The novel certifies his situation. It validates it, makes it concrete, gives it a name. Part of this is just reassurance, of course, and medicine does something similar. Something like this happens, for example, when a patient goes to psychiatrist and gets a diagnosis. It makes people feel better to have their illness named. To be able to say yes, I am a certified neurotic. I have an anxiety disorder.

But there is a radical difference between the way the novelist looks at the man who feels bad and doesn't know why and the way that medicine ordinarily does. Henderson the Rain King is going to look very different in the pages of Bellow's novel than he would in the *Journal of Nervous and Mental Diseases.* That difference is this: the medical standpoint looks at the man who feels bad and doesn't know why and says: This fellow is in bad shape.

What he needs is to develop his self-esteem, reconcile himself with his past, develop a meaningful relationship, get on a serotonin reuptake inhibitor. Whereas what the novel says, more often than not, is: Sure, this guy is in bad shape; and doesn't it look better than the alternative? The novel and the movie celebrate the man's predicament, in a perverse way. Sure, Tom More is a depressed, lust-ridden mental patient who drinks vodka with his grits, but who would you rather be: him, or his boring Presbyterian wife? The novel can say: Of course you're lonely and alienated and filled with terror and anxiety. Take a look around you; it would take a moron not to be. Percy says as much himself in *Lost in the Cosmos* when he writes: "You are depressed because you should be. You are entitled to your depression. In fact, you'd be deranged if you were not depressed. Consider the only adults who are never depressed: chuckleheads, California surfers and fundamentalist Christians who believe they have had a personal encounter with Jesus and are saved once and for all. Would you trade your depression to become any one of these?"[7]

What is going on here is what Percy calls elsewhere the "reversal of alienation by art," which is not exactly a cure for the alienated reader, but a way of identifying alienation and thereby turning it around. Not just certification, but what Binx Bolling only half-jokingly calls rotation and repetition, two terms Percy borrowed from Kierkegaard.

What is a repetition? A repetition is a way of reversing the everydayness by repeating the past. As Binx puts it, it is seeing a Western movie at the very same theater where he saw a Western fourteen years ago and feeling the camphor berries pop underneath his feet, just the same as they did years before, as a way of isolating and savoring the fourteen years that have elapsed. A repetition is like what Tom More in *Love in the Ruins* calls "historical therapy: a way of recapturing the past and thereby one's self."

A rotation, on the other hand, is what happened when I was trying to write this essay—and fully expecting to write it even though it was going very badly—when the power went off, and instead of writing it my wife and I found some candles and sat on the kitchen floor and drank Jack Daniels from the bottle. It is what Binx Bolling calls the "experiencing of the new beyond the expectation of experiencing the new." A trip to Niagara Falls on your honeymoon is not a rotation, or at least not much of a rotation, unless you happen to get lost, or have a wreck, or pick up a hitchhiker who turns out to be an escaped prisoner, in which case you would have had a kind of rotation that only happens in the movies. A rotation is not exactly a stroke of good fortune, but rather an event that has the effect of dispelling the malaise in which you have found yourself stuck. A rotation is often a journey—

Huck Finn on the river, Kerouac on the road—but not necessarily; the point of a rotation is not simply new experience but the transformation of experience beyond the expectation: like Gregor Samsa waking up one morning and finding that he is a giant beetle. The ultimate rotation is amnesia, where your past is forgotten and *everything* is new: where the everydayness of life disappears because there is no memory of the everyday. Percy uses a rotation similar to this in *The Last Gentleman,* where Bill Barrett lapses in and out of fugue states and sometimes comes to himself on old Civil War battlefields with no memory of how he got there.

Now my reason for dwelling on this is the way that repetition and rotation can be transmitted, as Percy says, through the novel or the movie. For example, one of my most memorable exercises in rotation and repetition was in Scotland when I saw Ross McElwee's film *Sherman's March.* First, the very title promised rotation: a journey. And not just any journey; the very journey of journeys, one with almost mythical resonance for southerners: Sherman's march to the sea. A journey by William Tecumseh Sherman, known to many (white) southerners as the Yankee devil himself. But this wouldn't be a rotation, of course, except for something that Ross McElwee, the narrator, tells the moviegoer at the beginning of the film. He says that he has been funded to make a documentary on Sherman's march—but it is pretty clear that this isn't what he is doing. Whatever the film is, it is not a documentary on Sherman's march. It's a fellow pacing around in an empty room talking apologetically to a camera. So a rotation is being set up: the experience of the new beyond the expectation of it. And not only that, we are set up for a repetition within a rotation: this is an expatriate southerner in the North, preparing for a journey back home.

And this is what we get: a homeward journey, a retracing of Sherman's march, and in the process, a set of off-kilter encounters with southern women, many of whom seem slightly deranged. And for me, the moviegoer, it was an unexpected repetition. There I sat, an expatriate southerner living in Scotland, watching a movie about another expatriate southerner with a Scottish name going back to the South, a man who happens to be from Charlotte, North Carolina, not twenty miles from my hometown, and moreover whose journey takes him to Charleston, South Carolina, thereby certifying the city where I once lived and only recently departed. By the time the movie ended I had been rotated, repeated, and certified.

Now even though I find Ross McElwee's films and Walker Percy's novels deeply satisfying, for reasons not unlike what Percy calls the reversal of alienation by art, I will confess that it is slightly misleading to call them therapeutic. Or at least to call them therapeutic in the same way that Prozac is. Prozac and the existential novel do different things, and I think this difference may get at some of the worries that many people have about the use of psychopharmacology in the way that Peter Kramer describes.

Occasionally I see book jacket blurbs for Percy's books that say something to the effect that he is a keen observer of the human condition, or that his books tell us something about what it is to be human. I think this gets things slightly wrong. I don't think Percy is trying to say something about the human condition so much as he is trying to say something about being a human being in the West in the twentieth century. And what he is trying to say is related to something that Charles Taylor writes about in his book *Sources of the Self.*[8]

Taylor writes that all human beings live within a certain framework of understanding that gives sense to their actions and to their lives. These are understandings about what sort of lives have dignity, what counts as a successful life and what counts as a failure, what kind of life is worth living and when a life has meaning. In other times and other cultures, a person might worry about her life being a failure *within* a given framework of understanding—about failing to meet the demands of her station in life, or of losing her honor, or of failing to live a life that will get her admitted into heaven, or displeasing her ancestors, and so on. Sometimes we feel some of these demands ourselves. But twentieth-century westerners face another problem: not that of failing to meet the demands of one's framework, like a southern gentleman who backs down from a duel, but that of being unsure of what the framework is. This is an altogether new and scary kind of feeling, a feeling that Taylor compares to vertigo: a sense of imbalance, because not only don't you know what kind of life to live; you don't know what, if anything, can tell you.

This feeling appears to people in different ways—vertigo, absurdity, emptiness, the malaise—and when we try to articulate it, we ask questions such as: Is this all there is? What is the sense of life? How does it all fit together? But Percy puts his finger on the way the question appears to many of us, which is: What am I supposed to be doing? This is not idle philosophizing; it is a practical question about action: Who am I supposed to be, and what am I supposed to do next? Percy's characters are more often than not southerners who don't really fit in the South. Sometimes they get a kind of nostalgia, or false nostalgia, for the old antebellum South, the stoic South where their grandfathers lived, not because they ever knew those times or even think they were especially enlightened but because at least then honor was honor and sin was sin and a person knew where he stood. Lance Lamar says he has no use for that kind of brutality, but maybe it's better to die with Stonewall Jackson at Chancellorsville than to live with Johnny Carson in Burbank.

Taylor develops a concept that he calls "strong evaluation."[9] Strong evaluation, says Taylor, is not about what we happen to prefer or have an interest in, but about what we think that people would be the worse for not preferring or having an interest in. So whereas I might enjoy sour-mash whiskey, might even enjoy it a lot, I don't think that a person ought to like it, or that he would be worse off if he preferred gin. On the other hand, I might well think worse of a person, or think that he is worse off, if I find that, for example, he likes to hunt endangered species, or if he simply can't stand listening to music of any sort. I once heard Pauline Kael say on the radio that she could not be friends with anyone who liked the movie *Forrest Gump*. This is a kind of strong evaluation.

I think this notion of strong evaluation may be hovering in the background of the Prozac debate. Those of us who are all too familiar with the malaise may feel somehow, like Binx, that we are onto something. Maybe not something happy, exactly, and not something that we would wish on others, but something reasonable and worth attending to, so that the idea of trying to do away with it seems questionable. Perhaps the old frameworks of meaning *are* disappearing, and this sense of malaise is a natural response. If so, then it is not unreasonable to feel as if we ourselves, and maybe even others, might be the worse for not having felt this way. Some kinds of responses to the world are reasonable even when they are disturbing.

Maybe the kind of feelings that Percy identifies—everydayness, the malaise, the ravening particles that suck the life out of the air for Will Barrett—are not so much symptoms of pathology as clues to a predicament. And if you are in a predicament, then the proper response will look less like treatment than like a search. As Binx says, "To become aware of the possibility of the search is to be onto something. Not to be onto something is to be in despair." Which is not to say that being lost and empty and puzzled is a good thing. But simply because it is not a good thing does not mean that it is a symptom of pathology. Not all problems are medical problems, and not all predicaments are neuroses. Which may be what keeps at least some people in predicaments from embracing antidepressants. For all the good that antidepressants do, there remains the nagging suspicion that many of the things they treat are in fact a perfectly sensible response to the strange times in which we live.

Notes

1 Some of the patients Kramer describes are in fact clinically depressed, however, and I should clarify that these are not the patients I have in mind for this essay. I do not want to call into question the use of serotonin reuptake inhibitors for major depression.
2 Peter Kramer, *Listening to Prozac* (London: Fourth Estate, 1994), 93.
3 Ibid., 146.
4 Ibid., 224.
5 Walker Percy, "Physician as Novelist," in *Signposts in a Strange Land,* ed. Patrick Samway (New York: Farrar, Straus and Giroux, 1991), 194.
6 To be fair, I should point out that Kramer discusses not *Love in the Ruins* but *The Thanatos Syndrome,* where Percy's message is somewhat different, and a bit more heavy-handed.
7 Walker Percy, *Lost in the Cosmos* (New York: Washington Square Press, 1983), 79.
8 Charles Taylor, *Sources of the Self* (Cambridge, Mass.: Harvard University Press, 1989), 18.
9 Charles Taylor, "A Most Peculiar Institution," in *World, Mind and Ethics: Essays on the Ethical Philosophy of Bernard Williams,* ed. J. E. J. Altham and Ross Harrison (Cambridge: Cambridge University Press, 1995), 134.

Ethics in the Ruins

David Schiedermayer

"First, reader and especially my fellow physicians, let me set forth my credentials," says Dr. More in *Love in the Ruins*. And then he talks about how his period of decline was also a period of "lying fallow" and of the "germination of strange quirky ideas."

I know the feeling.

I have just finished writing a poetry book. As Rafael Campo, a gay Cuban-American physician, noted in an interview, poetry is an "anti-credential in medicine."[1] I feel I need to set forth my credentials to prove that I am still a physician. Mostly I spend my time in clinic, or making rounds, or doing house calls, trying to keep patients alive at a time when even the patients talk about physician-assisted suicide. "The patient in DTs is asking us to kill him," my resident tells me. Have delirious alcoholics always talked this way?

My career is stalled out. I am being parked in the primary-care clinic. Even there, I must cope with the little ethical compromises that worsen my natural bent, pull my life off course even more. It is so bad that I consider taking Prozac or Paxil to kill the pain with something safer than alcohol. Every day, every day, every day, I perseverate, like the man with Alzheimer's who calls to the nurses in an Aqua-Lung voice, "Come here, come here, come here . . . cough, cough, cough."

The struggle is so pervasive that I suppose I will never make a discovery like Percy's More, hampered as I am by the pressure of all these ordinary ethical problems. But I am hoping it is a fallow time. I am working against some kind of gradient. If someone comes in complaining of dizziness, I say, dizziness, eh? and look out the window. Or I think, Hi Dee Hi Dee Hi Dee Ho, Hi Dee Hi Dee Hi Dee Hey. And then, like some office-based character in a Percy novel, I sink low enough in my chair so that we can talk to each other along the floor. Still, that is the right way to make the diagnosis in dizziness, isn't it? Ask the question, then sink low, listen, and write down the exact words the patient says? The CT scans and Holter monitors are mostly negative. The patient just feels out of balance, like the world is spinning away.

On my worst days I think of the review that John Lantos and I wrote of *The Thanatos Syndrome*. I hope this does not reflect poorly on the review. We published it in the *New England Journal of Medicine* some years ago. I think of it because I really think it wants to come true in medicine, in my own life, and I want to resist it or at least recognize that it is happening.

We wrote:

Imagine getting a call from a prestigious investigator who asks you to help coordinate a multi-dollar, multi-center drug trial. He recognizes the value of the brain isotope research you did before the years and the alcohol took their toll and you were sent to prison for selling amphetamines to truckers. You are just out of prison and could use the work. Imagine that the preliminary studies, which involved the covert addition of a heavy sodium isotope to a community's drinking water, demonstrated that heavy sodium reduces crime by 85%, neurosis by 79%, and AIDS by 76%. It also results in a 20% increase in IQ.

To participate or not to participate? Psychiatrist Tom More, "an old fashioned physician of the soul," is initially tempted to work on the project. After all, he wonders, if one can prescribe a chemical and turn a haunted psyche into a happy body, why take on a therapeutic quest for the root of the trouble, the heart of darkness? But the subtle behavioral changes he recognizes in his patients, his friends, and his wife—all exposed to heavy sodium—make him vaguely uneasy. He notes a clinical syndrome: "In each there has been a sloughing away of the old terrors, worries, rages, a shedding of guilt like last year's snakeskin, and in its place is a mild fond vacancy, a species of unfocused animal good spirits. Then are they . . . not better rather than worse? The answer is unclear."

Other questions begin to trouble More. What about informed consent? What harm might result from long-term exposure to the isotope? What does the project director really have in mind? Where will the project lead?

The reader comes to share More's apprehensions. Percy gradually brings More—and us—to face questions of our own autonomy, accountability, and spirituality. In Percy's view, we must choose between an immensely powerful science dedicated to improving the world, and an enigmatic religious conception of human frailty and imperfection embodied in Father Smith, an aging, decrepit priest. Father Smith confesses, during a seizure-induced utterance, that during a visit to Germany in the 1930's he was fascinated by the ideology of the Nazis. The priest puts the heavy-sodium experiment into moral context; he knows that like programs of eugenics and euthanasia, it represents the desire to purify Das Volk.

In *The Thanatos Syndrome,* the temptations of personal and professional ambition, which lead us to imagine that small ethical compromises can be justified by the larger ends they serve, are likened to the temptations of the scientific world view, wherein all the ills and sufferings of mankind are seen to have biochemical solutions. Physicians are particularly susceptible to both forms of temptation, Percy warns. If they succumb, they reduce ethical and spiritual problems to problems of compliance with their own technological prescriptions.[2]

Autonomy, accountability, spirituality.

Patient 1

I am staffing a ward team, and one of our patients, a twenty-year-old, obese African American woman, is ten weeks pregnant and has a huge saddle pulmonary embolus—a blood clot in her lung. She came up from the ER with the incorrect diagnosis of pneumonia, since she was coughing up blood, not pus, and she had the kind of terrible chest pain characteristic of an embolus. She is on intravenous heparin.

She would require intramuscular heparin throughout pregnancy if she wished to keep the baby, because coumadin is said to cause harm to the fetus. She requests an abortion, which she says she was planning on the very day she had the pulmonary embolus. She had an appointment.

Our intern is also African American, an associate pastor at his Baptist church, and he talks with her about options other than the procedure. I talk with her, too, later on in the afternoon. She won't hear of any other options. She has a twenty-month-old child already, same father, and although the man is opposed to the abortion, he agrees that she can do what she wants. All of us agree that she can do what she wants. Her mind is made up. The ethics consultation team agrees with her right to do what she wants, and they write this in the chart.

The obstetricians do the abortion the next day, and I see her in the afternoon. She has a little bleeding but otherwise feels well.

Now I suppose I should say here that I am morally opposed to abortions (I guess I should say religiously deeply opposed to abortion), but I can't justify withdrawing from her case. She is sick, with a life-threatening clot in her lung. She needs a general doc. Short of coercion (which I consider morally hideous), I could find no way to prevent this abortion. It is the law. It is her right. There is even a medical indication, a life-threatening clot requiring three to six months of anticoagulation to prevent her from dying.

I sit down for a moment in her room. The Bible is on her bed stand. I don't feel guilty or ashamed, and she doesn't either; you can see it. But I do feel somehow as if I have avoided something, as if I have turned my eyes away, turned my eyes away, turned my eyes away.

Patient 2

At his son's request, I stop the oxygen on a dying patient who has suffered a large stroke. The patient is breathing on his own on a general medical floor. The patient dies in less than five minutes. I did not know he needed the oxygen so much. If I had given him a lethal injection, it is doubtful he would have died so quickly. I sit at the nurse's station, and the patient's son comes and shakes my hand, my intern's hand, and says thank you. The nurses murmur.

Patient 3

An elderly man who is depressed asks me to help him die. I have him up on the psych unit, and even after four weeks of treatment with Serzone, he still wants to die. I think of the physician-assisted suicide laws, of the changes that are happening, and I say, I can't do that. Not yet. Not here. The next day, I try to persuade him that he needs a dog—an eight-year-old lab, say, with a big wide head, who will sit by him in his easy chair. Or a cat who craves affection, who will purr in his lap. He thinks about it for a while. Maybe, he says.

Patient 4

I consult on a ventilator-dependent quadriplegic man who refuses to be weaned so that he might die more easily when his ventilator is stopped. He is looking for a physician who is willing to stop his ventilator. The spinal cord unit physicians refuse to do this. In addition, the patient requests that he not be suctioned once the ventilator is removed. I offer to see him, but it is a mistake. The moment I see him, I realize I can't do what he wants. He doesn't have his talking trach in, but I don't have to hear what he says. He whispers, Help me, come back later, but I know I just can't stop his ventilator. I can't accept him in transfer.

But my friend does, without any real qualms. The patient dies two days after the withdrawal of the ventilator, with a high fever and an aspiration pneumonia. I wonder if I am missing something here. Is there a problem? Is there something wrong? Was I wrong to think there is something wrong? I look for someone to ask, but I don't know who will give me an unbiased opinion. Is this assisting a suicide or not?

My hope is that many of these ethical problems can be better faced through the use of poetry and prayer. When I write poetry, I feel as if I can capture what is really going on in the case. I feel less as if I need to take Prozac or Paxil. I feel less as if I have to uphold a tradition that is being eroded, less as if I am one of the last guardians of the Hippocratic Corpus. I feel more like a general doctor who is able to make new discoveries about the resilience of the soul. That is also what I feel when I pray. I feel the burden lift a little when I realize that I am rejecting the immense power of science and embracing an enigmatic religious conception of human dependence.

I think I can ask for a little help here.

Since I have discovered the clinical therapeutic benefit of poems and prayers I feel less impaired. Even if it is an anti-credential to admit that I write poems and pray, I like the sense that I have stopped depriving words of real meaning, in fact, that I am doing the opposite, I am giving words back their meaning. Sometimes I even pray with patients, and they almost always cry. Why?

Patient 5

> *Skin for Ricky*
> Your ear is mashed flat
> against your head
> your neck contorted
> in a tight C.
> You have such severe spastic Cerebral Palsy
> that you are almost quadriplegic
> and we must estimate your height
> by your wingspan,
> 183 cm.
>
> Now, as a 30 year-old
> your parents care for you
> in the living room.
> It is a full-time job.
>
> Once when you were in agony
> I gave you a GI cocktail—

Mylanta, viscous Xylocaine, Donnatol—
right down the stomach tube.
Your facial spasms eased.
Your moans stopped.

Ricky, I know you are
in there because I have seen
you ogle the young woman
who is working with me
(my medical student)
and I know a lecherous look
when I see one.

Your parents seemed surprised
(they turned on Nickelodeon)
but I was not.
You have CP, not dementia.
You know what nice smooth skin
looks like.

I do not condone lust
especially in others
but in your case
I might make an exception.

I might, if I were a young woman doctor
let my breasts brush over your face
as I listened to your lungs.

Maybe I would let my hair sweep
across your chest
as I listened to your heart.

It could be I would do this because I know
your heart is beating there
just somewhere
to the left
in your twisted rib cage

I might do this
even if I find it repugnant.
It would be an act of conscience.

More likely, I suppose
I would recoil from you
if I sensed your sexual desire.

Still, somehow I am sorry
that the only bare skin
you'll see from me
is my bald spot.[3]

The general doc is now in the third person as he walks from the county hospital to the medical school. John Anderson is a first-year medical student interested in ethics. He wanted to do something in ethics for the summer and applied for a stipend to do a project on the physician and the theater. His application cited the general doc's work so fondly that it was ego-dystonic not to help John write the proposal. The school has funded the proposal and will give John $1,500 to study the physician and the theater.

John is waiting in the office when the general doc returns from the clinic. They talk about ethics for a while, about the need to begin work on an article, and about the conference poster that is required at the end of the project. The general doc, who is not exactly an authority on the theater, wonders who would be able to help lend credibility to the article. Someone with the time and money and culture really to understand the theater. One of the deans is such a person. The general doc puts him on the list of people to call. But all of them are too busy, and in the end, the general doc works on the article with the student, and they get it published after all. The student is still a friend.

Hours pass, and another student, Ann Harrison, is sitting in the general doc's office. She wants to do a project surveying nursing homes. The doc puts in a call to a colleague who has already done the survey.

The general doc has just finished chairing the ethics committee meeting. The committee is drafting policy on advance directives to be in line with the recently approved durable power of attorney. As chairman, he has learned the strengths and weaknesses of each member. They have recently put on a conference that was attended by two hundred people from throughout the region. The feedback on the conference was good, especially the comment that said that for the price, the content and speakers were excellent.

The conference was free.

The general doc and his colleague are being interviewed by a television crew about the topic of CPR in the elderly and about living wills and durable powers of attorney. The lights are blindingly bright. The general doc's tie is slightly crooked, and his sleeves are too short. He feels highly uncomfortable and wishes ethics weren't such a media honey pot. Will the viewers switch channels when he speaks?

The general doc sits with another one of his several bosses. They are writing a very complex grant together. It is one in a series of long grants. They write well together, and the proposal seems sound. Now they must wait for the answer, which in all statistical likelihood will be no.

> Three jobs for the Department Chiefs under the sky
> Seven jobs for the Division Heads in their halls of stone
> Nine jobs for Associate Professors doomed to die
> One job for the Dean on his swivelling throne
> In the land of Medschool where the shadows lie
> One job to rule them all, one job to find them
> One job to bring them all and in contracts bind them
> In the land of Medschool where the shadows lie.

He is an associate professor, the general doc is, so he has a number of conflicting jobs. One of them is taking care of a VIP's father. He is eighty-nine years old, and has been in excellent health all his life, except for the last six months, since he has become the general doc's patient. Now he is deteriorating, and the general doc has been forced to hospitalize him. He has more notes on the chart than the junior medical student. He personally brings the patient some towels and adjusts his bed. The workup reveals a colon tumor. This is a man who has been healthy all his life.

The general doc wants to write a novel. He does not have the right personality for it, of course, but he will not let that stop him. If it is humanly possible, he will do it, even if it is a bad novel. He must take the next step, from poetry to the novel, because he thinks if poetry is healing, then a novel must be absolutely invigorating. If prayer is good, then prayer and fasting must be better.

But like poetry, when he sits down to write, it still seems like work. Someone said writing is easy—just sit down and open a vein. But writing does not cause real bleeding. The general doc knows what real bleeding can do to you, the kind of bleeding that happens when you read the *Wall Street Journal* more than your medical journals, when you worry more about your retirement accounts than your patients, when you think more about money than sex and more about food than friends.

Now that is audible bleeding, the kind that comes out of nicked major arteries during botched surgery, and that kind of bleeding should make you nervous. A little bleeding on the printed page actually helps prevent iron overload.

It is late afternoon. The general doc is tired. In his office is an extraordinarily beautiful young woman whom he knows has recently been divorced. She has a problem with ethical overtones, and she is seeking his advice. She is a staff physician, and she has fallen in love with one of the residents. She is this resident's small-group clinical teacher, and she will be responsible for training him for the next six months.

How did you meet him, the general doc asks. That's the funny thing, the woman says. I met him at a party and was attracted to him right away. We talked for an hour, and he never mentioned his work—neither did I. When I saw him again, I felt something move inside, a real passion. He is older than the other residents—my age.

The general doc says they can date, if the following criteria are met:

1. Try to transfer the resident to another service.

2. No evaluation of the resident by this staff.

3. The staff should explain the relationship to the other residents in the small group and make it clear that no evaluation is occurring.

Thank you, says the woman. Thank you very much. The general doc looks up to see if she is being ironic, looks her right in the face. She is happy.

It is twilight now. The general doc looks at the walls in his office. He looks at the stacks of envelopes and papers on his desk. He recently sent a priest for a Whipple procedure. The man had come in with jaundice, and a CT showed a pancreatic mass. The priest had been overly kind to the ward team, thanking them for their participation in his care, literally getting out of bed to speak with them during rounds. The general doc sees a letter with the pathology report and opens it:

Head of pancreas, duodenum, and omentum:

1. Poorly differentiated invasive pancreatic adenocarcinoma with mucinous differentiation.

2. Tumor present in a single peripancreatic lymph node.

3. Tumor invading bowel wall with intraluminal extension.

4. Small bowel margin of resection negative for tumor.

5. Pancreatic margin positive for tumor in the pancreatic bed.

6. The pancreatic margins of resection contain tumor less than 1 mm from the margin, and focal tumor cells at the inked margin.

7. Sections from the margin of resection line in the pancreas are also notable for a small focus of venous invasion by tumor.

The general doctor closes the envelope and puts it back on the pile. He works on writing this essay, and he looks at Walker Percy's picture on the back of his hardcover copy of *The Thanatos Syndrome*. Percy has a sad smile, a wide nose, some aging spots on his cheeks and forehead. It is an excellent photo. He wears a dark shirt, with a herringbone jacket, brown belt, and corduroy pants. Percy does not look like a doctor; he looks like a novelist. He looks fairly well rested.

The general doc sighs. He has been putting on weight lately; his eyes have bags under them; he is starting to look like the old Norwegians and Germans he used to meet at his family reunions. He does not look like a novelist. He is jealous of Percy's escape from medicine. Crichton also left, so did Cook, many others. William Carlos Williams stayed in, as did John Stone.

Maybe the anti-credential is the secret if you want to stay in. Maybe if you write enough poetry, doctors will figure you are just eccentric, and they will ignore you. Then you will be able to keep on being a doctor and keep on writing. But you will have to write in your spare time, in your office, after a full day, with someone's lab and path reports spread out around you like the landscape spreads in front of the beginning landscape artist. You will be seen as an awkward beginner, a novice, no matter how hard you try, because you are still a doctor.

You will still have to tell the priest that the surgeons did not get it all. You will have to send him for chemotherapy, and soon enough he will be so sick that he won't be able to get out of bed to greet you.

The general doc picks up his poetry book. He looks at the back cover. It is blank. He sighs, thinking of how he much he wanted the Whipple to work. The patient passed the nice guy test. That is why he has to die.

The general doc is asked to head up some of the clinics and educational programs at his school. He prays, talks with his wife and friends. Autonomy, accountability, spirituality.

He tells them that this is a wonderful opportunity. He could move on to be a chief somewhere. It will look good on his résumé. He will have power, real power. He will have some budget line-item control. His career will be jump-started. Saying no to this will be difficult. They tell him to say no.

He tells his chief and goes home. On his way out, he tells his secretary that he will not be in the next morning. He is going to the Schlitz Audubon nature center with his son to watch the geese walk on the path. He will ride the bus both there and back.

It is a long trip on the bus with thirty children. It will take time, much time, and he will not think at all of the hospital or the medical school or power of any kind or the prevalence of pancreatic cancer or of *The Thanatos Syndrome.* He will bring along a large pretzel. He will put it in his mouth like he used to when he smoked a few cigars in Chicago. He will squint his eyes a little and look out the window of the bus. He will pray to resist the power, which will try to reach him even here. He will think about writing several poems. And it will be a sunny day, an unusually clear and sunny day for Wisconsin at that time of year.

Notes

1 Z. Ingalls, "A Professor of Medicine Discovers the Healing Power of Poetry," *Chronicle of Higher Education,* 28 February 1997, sec. B, pp. 8–9.

2 David Schiedermayer and John Lantos, "Review: *The Thanatos Syndrome,*" *New England Journal of Medicine* 317 (1987): 254.

3 David Schiedermayer, "Skin for Ricky," in *House Calls, Rounds, and Healings: A Poetry Casebook* (Tucson, Ariz.: Galen Press, 1996), 7–8.

Walker Percy and Medicine

The Struggle for Recovery in Medical Education

Richard Martinez

If the reader is, like Binx, in need of God, he will see in Percy's writing the sign of grace. If the reader is a scientific humanist, he probably will not, but he still may appreciate the good story. —Linda Whitney Hobson

By all accounts, Walker Percy was a private man. He was humble, while shrewd and commanding in intelligence. In a day, he would write resting in bed, have lunch with his wife and children, and perhaps spend some time bird-watching or playing golf. A visit with friends to Bechacs was not uncommon. In the evening, Percy could be found sitting on his porch, sipping a little bourbon as the sun faded and the sky turned crimson. From the work of Jay Tolson [1] and Robert Coles,[2] one gets the sense that Walker Percy created a life where waiting, watching, and listening were valued priorities, necessary for the emergence of the wonderment and mystery found in his essays and novels.

I have studied and read the writings on and about Walker Percy for more than twenty years. Those who had the good fortune to know Dr. Percy, to sit and visit with him in Covington, discuss and reflect, listen and watch the quiet of the Bogue Falaya River, and smell the honeysuckle, have left a valuable record of the man's life and mind. I admire the curiosity and perseverance that brought them to his door. These wayfarers include intellectuals and students, theologians, lovers of good books, historians, photographers, journalists, literary critics, physicians, the occasional ornithologist and naturalist, writers and essayists, wayward Jesuits, and all sorts of other folks who, like myself, turn to Walker Percy's stories, essays, and life for signs, for messages.

But with Walker Percy, one soon discovers that although the messages left along the path are generous, intelligent, and well crafted, to decipher hidden meanings and intentions requires a willingness to struggle. My effort to meet him in 1990, the year of his illness and death, was not successful. Even in that last year, he returned a note to me, stating his decision to not give another interview, but he provided references to previous interviews. I regret that I waited so long to request a meeting.

The Message in the Bottle

The existential modes of human living . . . can be derived only from . . . one man encountering another man, speaking a word, and through it and between them discovering the world and himself. —Walker Percy

Walker Percy stated that the "shout in silence" was the best method to deliver "good news." With eclectic interests, a bad habit of avoiding the difficult, and a strange search of my own that has led me from literature to medical school, to psychiatry and psychoanalysis, then back to literature and the teaching of medical ethics and humanities, I now require skeptical, for the most part scientific empiricists and humanists—also called medical students—to read the work of Walker Percy in a course entitled "Literature, Medicine, and Ethics."

In such teaching, the challenge is to help students see what Walker Percy might offer them in their journey of becoming doctors. No easy task when one is reminded that *The Moviegoer* was written by a physician-writer who never practiced medicine, developed hostility toward science and its objective posture, was preoccupied throughout his adult life with a nonbiological theory of humankind and human consciousness, converted to Catholicism, and for the most part had a nasty attitude toward experts and professionals.

The invitation to write an essay on Walker Percy excited me. But what could I say about teaching the work of a man who has played and continues to play such a large part in my own search? In my years of teaching literature to medical and premedical students, Percy's work is often the most difficult for students to understand. Students sometimes complain about the requirement of reading his work. His stories, they argue, don't tell them things that are "helpful in becoming doctors." They say, "I don't get it. What's this search got to do with medicine? I don't get this Binx character. He's lost, he mistreats women." Or I hear, "Dr. More is crazy. What if you don't believe in Christianity? What can he say to me?"

"I'm not sure," I say. "I don't have the answers. I know half of you don't like to read him and don't get it and don't care to get it. I know some of you don't get it but tell me there's something there you might get, someday. And I know some of you love his work, and think you get it, sometimes." I try to reassure. "Just try to hang in with it. Perhaps something will speak to you." I look up to some corner of the classroom, grow silent. I wait. I listen to the quiet and watch. I drive home. I crawl into bed and open to Walker Percy's essay "Diagnosing the Modern Malaise":

> Then what is the task of serious fiction in an age when both the Judeo-Christian consensus and rational humanism have broken down? I suggest that it is more than the documentation of the loneliness and the varieties of sexual encounters of so much modern fiction. I suggest that it is nothing less than an exploration of the options of such a man. That is, a man who not only is in Crusoe's predicament, a castaway of sorts, but who is also acutely aware of his predicament. What did Crusoe do? He looked around. He explored the island. He scanned the horizon. He looked for signs from across the seas. He combed the beach—for what? Perhaps for bottles with messages in them. No doubt, he also launched bottles with messages in them. But what kind of messages? That is the question. The contemporary novelist . . . must know how to send messages and decipher them. The messages may come not in bottles but rather in the halting and muted dialogue between strangers, between lovers and friends. One speaks; the other tries to fathom his meaning—or indeed to determine if the message has any meaning.[3]

I was born in New Orleans and spent most of my early life there. As an undergraduate at Tulane University, I read three of Percy's novels. I found them disturbing yet comforting, but I could no more articulate the reasons for my reactions at that time than describe the feel and taste of the moon. During those years, I felt a certain uneasiness and confusion over whether to choose the path of writer and teacher of literature or to enter what I perceived to be the safer domain of medicine.

As an undergraduate student, I was torn between the abstractions of literature and philosophy on the one hand and, on the other, my feelings of excitement and curiosity when I visited Charity Hospital's emergency room with a family friend who was a pediatrician at the medical school. He performed spinal taps, talked to parents, and demonstrated great love for his work and the children within his care. Here was a man in the world, acting, committed to other human beings in an important way. Literature and Walker Percy went underground for the next five years while I went to medical school.

It wasn't long after medical school, while still a resident in psychiatry and in psychoanalysis, that I picked up a worn copy of *The Last Gentleman.* I was reminded of my earlier interests in Will Barrett and his purchase of a telescope with his last savings, savings intended for his psychoanalysis. Percy and his work began to take hold again. Binx Bolling and Will Barrett were joined by Dr. Tom More. Toward the end of my residency in psychiatry, steeped in the ideologies of medical psychiatry and psychoanalysis, Dr. Tom More and his exploits in *Love in the Ruins* reemerged and reminded me of why medicine and its culture disturbed me and left me wanting.

For years I had been engaged in the kind of journey that Walker Percy once embraced, a belief in scientific medicine, and I found comfort in the belief that such a worldview provided stability and order and solved problems. But as patient after patient sat before me, as I listened and watched, and the months turned to years, I saw the limitations of such a view. Like Binx Bolling waking in his Gentilly apartment, I realized a search was possible. I returned to *The Moviegoer, The Last Gentleman, Love in the Ruins,* and *The Message in the Bottle,* and before long, I was acquainted again with old friends. Percy's words in his essay "From Facts to Fiction" returned at this crucial time:

> If the first great intellectual discovery of my life was the beauty of the scientific method, surely the second was the discovery of the singular predicament of man in the very world which has been transformed by this science. An extraordinary paradox became clear: that the more science progressed, and even as it benefited man, the less it said about what it is like to be a man living in the world. Every advance in science seemed to take us further from the concrete here-and-now in which we live. Did my eyes deceive me, or was there not a huge gap in the scientific view of the world (scientific in the root sense of the word "knowing")? If so, it was an oversight which everyone pretended not to notice or maybe didn't want to notice.[4]

My patients could not be summed up in psychiatric diagnoses, placed on medication, and sent on their way. Psychotherapy itself, with its proscriptions and rituals, placed me at a distance from others, provided few clues of how to explore the existential and spiritual elements so important to most people. Struggles with trauma, depression, psychosis, guilt, isolation and loneliness, anger, sexual dissatisfaction — these can't be summed up so easily. The medicalization of psychiatry, the language of object relations theory and self-psychology, the endless disagreements on human cognitive and affective development, and the connection of development to borderline and narcissistic states — these abstractions began to dilute and drain the humanity from those many suffering individuals who came for my help.

Medicine and the Ordeal of Illness

It takes an awful lot of ordeal . . . these days to come to a sense of self. It doesn't do any good to be told how to live, and it doesn't do any good to tell yourself how to live. You have to learn it yourself, through ordeal. And the language fails, unless you do it by ordeal. — Walker Percy to Linda Whitney Hobson

The ship of medicine is a continuous rotation, a roll in the sea of love and death, the chronic condition of ordeal, with a bit of episodic amnesia thrown on board in order to endure. After all, how can one be surrounded by such ordeal—of death, madness, and sickness—without checking out? Psycho-analysis was my Kierkegaardian repetition, a return to the home of my youth. As Walker Percy understood, some repetitions are helpful in the movement toward responsibility and commitment, but some are dead ends.

My own psychoanalysis, in spite of its focus on the individual and the indi-vidual's personal history, remained primarily an aesthetic pursuit. It helped me identify my likes and dislikes, and to better appreciate those aspects of myself that burdened and limited my desires. My wants and needs in the material aspect of living a life were extended. But the experience did not en-gage my deeper search. Psychoanalysis, with its tradition of objectivity and practice rituals that minimize intersubjective discovery, did not adequately address concerns about myself as a moral agent, as a spiritual creature, as a man wishing to contribute, trying to grapple with despair, meaning, and love. Psychoanalysis can be what Walker Percy called "the guru's search within" rather than "the pilgrim's search outside himself."[5] Like Will Barrett, I needed my own telescope, my own way of seeing things. I left psychoanaly-sis and embarked on a different kind of search.

I continued to experience confusion about the purposes, meanings, and aspirations involved in my choices as a doctor. Medicine practiced without reflection on the spirit, or the question of meaning, or the mystery of the intersubjective domain, and professional life that fails to promote awareness of being-in-the-world while of the world, that defeats the desire to "hand" each other "along"; such a life leaves one with a very incomplete journey and solution. Walker Percy's "theorist-consumer" description of our age can be seen in the modern practice of medicine. This modern practice lacks compassion, discounts individual suffering and pain, and turns professional life into compartmentalized "role" behavior in which the professional's per-sonal values and aspirations are minimized and discouraged.

To treat the illness of the other requires one to treat one's own illness, to acknowledge one's own despair, boredom, detachment and disconnection, and tendency toward the scientific objectification of the other. Medicine can seduce. In medicine, professionals pursue enlivened and ecstatic selves while, not uncommonly, the experience of alienation, distance, and aloneness grows. Professionals lose sight of the ideals and aspirations that once motivated their desire to become doctors, nurses, or other health care professionals. Caricatures from television medical heroes replace authentic concern for the suffering of others. The medical gaze, with its effect of reducing human suffering and experience of illness to diseases that are probed, diagnosed, and treated, worried Dr. Percy. This concern became the subject of much of his diagnosing of the modern and postmodern age in his essays and novels.

Struggling to master the information necessary to become a doctor subverts and discourages the exploration of meaning and purpose. Professional power and detachment enable professionals to avoid themselves, to remain unaware of the tough and difficult questions that emerge after identity as a role has been exhausted. As Kierkegaard helped Walker Percy to see, the question of how to live and how to die is often too difficult to engage, yet too important to ignore. During Walker Percy's illness, his concerns shifted. "What began to interest me was not so much a different question as a larger question, not the physiological and pathological processes within man's body but the problem of man himself, the nature and destiny of man; specifically and more immediately, the predicament of man in a modern technological society."[6]

For the professional as well as the patient, this question sits before all medical encounters, waiting to be discovered, waiting to be ignored. For the patient, the ordeal, the illness, "the dangerous opportunity," as Arthur Frank writes in his illness memoir, begins a process.[7] After science is exhausted, the remains of the day require the professional and the patient to struggle for and wrench the meaning and purpose from the experience of ordeal. The professional, the doctor, as human being and individual, subject to the same mortality, frailty, and vulnerability as the patient whom she diagnoses and treats, must recognize her part in this suffering. If she is "to come to herself," the occasion must be an opportunity for understanding, through a relationship to her patient, of herself as self.

Modern Medicine in a Postmodern World

At its best our age is an age of searchers and discoverers, and at its worse, an age that has domesticated despair and learned to live with it happily.—Flannery O'Connor

A number of years ago, while climbing the volcano Popocatépetl in Mexico, I herniated a cervical disc in an accident. A Kierkegaardian rotation on my part turned into an ordeal that is still with me, with occasional paresthesias in my left arm, and neck stiffness. During my subsequent treatment and recovery, like William Hurt's surgeon-patient in the movie *The Doctor,* I experienced those aspects of medicine and the patient-physician relationship that can be seen best if the one who is a doctor becomes a patient. As did Walker Percy with his experience of illness, I used this malady as an opportunity to reflect on the limits, benefits, and harms of scientific medicine.

My "sports medicine" physician, a sensitive woman my own age, involved me fully in my care, always remained mindful of my discomfort, offered choices for treatment of pain, never tried to talk me out of what I was feeling, and was able to tolerate my condition while never acting overly responsible for me. As Anatole Broyard has written in his memoir about his illness with prostate cancer, my doctor did not need to suffer with me, but I did wish for her to "brood on my situation" when I was with her.[8] She explained the options for medical treatment. This included pain management, physical therapy, rest, massage, ultrasound stimulation, and a brace to extend the space between the cervical vertebrae. She explained as well the option of surgery. She presented the advantages and disadvantages of medical versus surgical treatment and encouraged me to see a surgeon for a second opinion.

The experience with the surgeon was a different matter. In discussing my diagnosis and treatment options, he was distant, aloof, professionally rigid, overly technical, and he had that youthful discomfort with my discomfort, trying to soothe by telling me, "It won't be that bad." I didn't fault the young doctor, but I was acutely aware of the disconnection. My desire to have someone acknowledge my fear and anxiety, to acknowledge my feelings, not diminish them or fix them, but simply be there, engaged and connected as I struggled with *my injury,* could not be found with this physician. After the MRI confirmed a herniation between my fifth and sixth cervical vertebrae with impingement on the nerve root to my left shoulder and arm, the surgeon stated his preference for surgery. He explained the procedure, which involved an anterior entrance through my neck, and stated that he was skeptical of a nonsurgical approach to my injury. I decided to return to my "medical" physician for "medical treatment." Eight months later, I returned to basketball, hiking, and other activities and, with some occasional minor setbacks, continue those activities.

Two physicians, two very different experiences, two different views of medicine, science, and the concept of the professional. Walker Percy understood the postmodern dilemma before such a term entered our common cultural lexicon. In his first published novel, *The Moviegoer,* Binx Bolling suffers the malaise of modernism, but it is malaise because of the failure of the modern project. The certainty of values and knowledge of modernism no longer hold. The traditional stoic, the secular romantic, the empirical scientist, and the materialist consumer are formulas available to Binx. But Binx is situated at the end of the modern. The dilemma of postmodern life requires a different solution if authenticity and hope are to replace alienation and despair. Whether or not we support Walker Percy's ultimate solution for this dilemma with his turn to Christianity, he offers us a series of protagonists such as Binx Bolling, who, as is the case with their progenitor Robinson Crusoe, are washed ashore and stranded, not on an island, but at the crossroads of modernism and postmodernism.

In my experience of injury, my first physician possessed qualities of the ethical postmodern professional. She respected me as an individual, not a disease. She approached the science of medicine as a tool to situate my particular suffering and injury but did not allow science to become the dominant perception to explain me or herself. Walker Percy's attempt to create a theory of human consciousness began with a disdain of the view of human being as "an organism in an environment." This view, a dominant image in medical science, is counter to the compassion and concern showed to me by my first physician. She understood my illness as my experience. She offered herself as a facilitator in my journey. And although it was never made explicit, my sovereignty over this injury experience was supported and encouraged.

As a professional, she approached me with elements of humility and acknowledged limits to her own knowledge about what might happen in the individual and local situation of my particular injury. This postmodern tolerance describes an ethical ideal for the practice of medicine and the activity of the professional. In postmodern medicine, despite the claim of potential nihilistic relativism, the culture of medicine embraces the patient's personal experience of illness and injury and the intersubjective element in determining. Ancient and traditional values that define medical practice are placed in tension with contemporary social construction of the goals and purposes of medicine. This tension introduces the humility and tolerance in medical practice that are necessary for the support of the patient's sovereignty over his or her experience. Medicine moves from a predominately aesthetic culture of scientific empiricism toward a moral enterprise.

The second physician practiced in the modern aesthetic of medicine. He perceived my injury and subsequent suffering as solely of the body, and therefore it was the body that needed to be probed and fixed. As with the Cnidian practitioners of ancient Greece, modern medicine concerns itself with diseases rather than persons. Practitioners of the modern period do not conceptualize their work as a moral enterprise. Scientific medicine objectifies me and my source of pain, and professional responsibility is limited to the role of diagnosing and fixing the mechanical failure of my body.

According to Arthur Frank in his book *The Wounded Storyteller,* in modernism, physicians "are responsible more to professional codes than to individual patients. According to modernist universalism, the greatest responsibility to all patients is achieved when the professional places adherence to the profession before the particular demands of any individual patient." This kind of professionalism "is responsible less to individual people than to truth, understood on several levels: the factual truth of medical science, the beneficent truth of institutional management in the hospital, and ultimately the political truth of administering people's welfare."[9]

Walker Percy understood that the human element disappears when modern scientific medicine with its emphasis on experts, technology, science, cure, and the denial of death determines behavior between the patient and the professional. Experts and professionals lose sight of the common bonds of frailty and mortality that connect human beings. Modernism means technical expertise and complex organizations of medical care. Medical language is the dominant story of illness, and professionalism is increasingly compartmentalized in narrower concepts of role, rules, and professional and clinical guidelines. In *The Wounded Storyteller,* Frank argues that postmodernism is the condition where "the accumulated violences of modernity are no longer deniable."[10] The goals of medicine and the patient's experience of illness, the definition of professional values and purposes of professionalism, and the ethical use of technology depend on finding the words, stories, and arguments that persuade toward the good and away from violence.

Walker Percy spent his creative life reminding us of the potential dangers of scientific rationalism as an aesthetic ideal. In his novels and essays, where the dangers of a "theorist-consumer" world are so intelligently described, he offers ways to bring the ethical and spiritual domain into medical education and medical practice.

Lionel Trilling cautioned: "We must be aware of the dangers which lie in our most generous wishes. Some paradox of our nature leads us, when once we have made our fellow men the objects of our enlightened interest, to go on to make them the objects of our pity, then of our wisdom, ultimately of our coercion."[11] Walker Percy understood this dark aspect of human nature. If we embrace Walker Percy's caution, even if it falls short of his "leap of faith," perhaps we are better off, a step back from the danger of objectification and the distant medical gaze supported by the instruments through which we probe and search.

Perhaps, with Walker Percy's help, we can remind students of the pleasure and wonderment that can be discovered through involvement and connection with others. With Walker Percy's help, students can examine their own notions of professionalism and expertise, of how one's personal beliefs and values are inseparable from professional life. Perhaps, with Walker Percy's help, we can remind our students that they are human beings first, doctors second, and that the patient is teacher through suffering always.

Rotation and Recovery

Every explorer names his island Formosa, beautiful. To him it is beautiful because, being first, he has access to it and can see it for what it is. But to no one else is it ever as beautiful—except the rare man who manages to recover it, who knows that it has to be recovered.—Walker Percy

In the essay "The Loss of the Creature," Walker Percy describes García López de Cárdenas's amazement at the discovery of the Grand Canyon.[12] Percy reflects on the fact that the modern world does not allow for the experience of the "creature" of a thing, the state of a thing being a thing. He argues that it is difficult for the modern traveler to see what de Cárdenas saw. Percy struggled with this problem of experience divorced from being. He struggled with the tension between the authentic and the inauthentic, the self being itself versus the self trying to be something it ought to be in a world in which nothing surprising can happen.

In today's world, you decide to visit the Grand Canyon. You go to your travel agent, see wonderful pictures of what you will see, then sign up for the vacation. You talk with your wife and children for weeks and months about what you'll see once you are there. Finally, the day of departure arrives. You and your family fly to Phoenix, then drive across the desert in a rented car. Or perhaps you join a tour. You arrive at the Bright Angel Trailhead, take photographs of all you see, perhaps hike about the park, stay overnight in the lodge or camp. You return home. Once home, you present a slide show of your trip to your friends. Walker Percy then reflects: "Why is it almost impossible to gaze directly at the Grand Canyon under these circumstances and see it for what it is—as one picks up a strange object from one's back yard and gazes directly at it?" Why is it so difficult to "see" objects of the world, to see the world itself as utterly unique, as if for the first time, as if in a trance of being with the object for the first time? What keeps us from seeing the canyon for the amazing thing that it is?

Walker Percy called this problem with seeing "preformulation," the packaging of the object by modern culture. The object, such as the Grand Canyon, can no longer be seen as the Spanish explorer saw the "creature" of the thing; it can be seen only as the object succeeds or fails in measuring up to some "preformed complex" of the object in the viewer's mind. Whereas de Cárdenas was able to experience delight from "the penetration of the thing itself, from a progressive discovery of depths, patterns, colors, shadows, etc.," the modern seer cannot see. In the modern world, the thing eludes us. Walker Percy argues that the task of the modern searcher is to recover the object, to see it fresh, alive, with wonderment and awe. To see in this way, the Grand Canyon must be seen again as the thing that it is. This requires that we free ourselves from this modern preformulation.

Walker Percy, borrowing from Kierkegaard, presents us with several strategies for recovering the "creature" element of experience. Rotation is one strategy for recovery. In *The Moviegoer,* Binx Bolling attempts several rotations. His moviegoing is a form of rotation. By going to the movies, Binx hopes to escape the malaise of his life. Binx defines a good rotation: "A good rotation. A rotation I define as the experiencing of the new beyond the expectation of the experiencing of the new. For example, taking one's first trip to Taxco would not be a rotation, or no more than a very ordinary rotation; but getting lost on the way and discovering a hidden valley would be."[13] As Binx later tells the reader, rotations are strategies to escape the grip of everydayness, with its inevitable boredom and potential for despair and alienation. The concept that the road is better than the inn describes rotation. It is better to be focused on what lies around the bend than on the stillness of the moment.

In medicine, health care professionals are involved continuously in rotational behavior. Medical experience is the seduction of the endless road. Although the emergency room physician and surgeon initially come to mind, all doctors are lovers of the new experience announced through the sound of the beeper. The practice of medicine provides a new rotation each and every day, a never-ending promise that the best is yet to come. When boredom and everydayness of activity creep into the physician's life, there is always the ability to pass the old responsibility on to the next generation of rotation-seeking enthusiasts. Pass it on to the resident, to the intern, to the medical student. Unfortunately, all too often, in the hierarchy of medical education and practice, what gets passed on is the opportunity to sit with the patient, to listen to the patient's story.

Medicine is ordeal, and in ordeal, there are many opportunities for the patient and the professional to engage or avoid the opportunity for inter-subjective discovery and wonderment. The medical gaze toward the patient, now extended with highly developed technologies that go far beyond the stethoscope, furthers the distance between seer and object and promotes the experience of the other as separate in the moral sense, and disconnected in the community sense. The "creature" of the person is lost. The doctor of the modern age chases technology as Binx chases his secretaries. And like Binx, after rolling in the sands of the Gulf Coast, the doctor of today is left confused and exhausted once he has mastered his technologies and discovers that he is blind to the person whose body he has probed and measured.

The Struggle for Recovery

As Mounier said, the person is not something one can study and provide for; he is something one struggles for. But unless he also struggles for himself, unless he knows that there is a struggle, he is going to be just what the planners think he is.
—Walker Percy

As a medical educator, I struggle to help students recover the "creature" in medical experience, in their patients, and in themselves. At the end of his essay, Walker Percy describes a young Falkland Islander walking along a beach and spying a dead dogfish in the sand. The young man goes to work on the shark with his jackknife, exploring and seeking. Percy then transports the reader to a biology class where students are asked to dissect a dogfish but have no ability to "see" in the way the Falkland Islander sees. Percy reminds us of the citizen in *Brave New World* who stumbles on a volume of Shakespeare in some vine-grown ruins, then sits and reads. Unlike the Harvard sophomore in English Poetry II, this citizen "sees" the work of Shakespeare.

Walker Percy reminds us that we cannot see a thing for what it is because of the packaging, the "preformulation." He suggests that the educational packaging prevents students from seeing. Walker Percy argues that students cannot recover the experience of the dogfish at Shreveport High, nor recover the sonnet from Shakespeare while sitting in the Harvard classroom, because of the educator's presentation of the object "as a lesson to be learned," rather than "as beings to be known." As it is with sonnets and dogfish, so too is it in every medical school with the human beings who are suffering with illness and injury while studied and examined by the medical profession. Individuals become lessons to be learned, not human beings to be discovered.

In my literature class in the medical school, I ask my students to read *The Moviegoer* after three-fourths of the semester has passed. By then, the vast majority of students have staked out their chairs around the table. Being the creatures that we are, most of the students settle into a pattern of seating themselves between particular friends. When we are in the middle of struggling with the concept of rotation, I ask that each student look to the left and right, study the face of his or her neighbors, the clothes they are wearing, the color of their eyes and hair, the shape of their face. I then ask them to look across to the folks on the opposite side of the table, and then to the objects arranged around the room. This takes a couple of minutes at most. I then ask them to move to another seat. They can sit anywhere else in the room, but they cannot sit next to a person who previously occupied a position to their left or right.

I ask that they look around again, observe their new neighbors, and observe the room again from their new position. This exercise is always illuminating. I explain that we have participated in a rotation. It is a good rotation if their new position is better than anticipated, and a not so good rotation if they long to be back in their previous chair. The discussion that follows is always powerful. One young medical student tells of her discomfort now sitting across from me and away from her friend. She felt "safer" next to me. Another states that she "feels different," more awake and alert. One student reports "seeing" objects in the room, previously unseen, and notices other students differently. I then direct them to reexamine Binx's experience of rotation. The students, at least most of them, appreciate what Walker Percy is trying to show through the character of Binx Bolling. They reflect on their instinctive tendency to sit in the same chair week after week, of their failure to create new perspectives and new opportunities to see, and of their longing to preserve and nurture wonderment in their own seeing.

Then comes the hard part of the exercise. I ask, "How many times each day do you seek a new perspective? Is this change in perspective something you do consciously, reflexively, or reflectively? Is there value in being conscious of such seeking?" And then, "What if you cannot change perspective, you must stay in your original position, yet still re-create the wonderment of being as if in the new position?"

Binx Bolling realizes that there are no new chairs to occupy. Rotations are exhausted, moviegoing at an end; he chooses the inn, not the road. He commits to those who are before him, with their fears and imperfections. He commits to the position and perspective that has been offered. Binx Bolling decides to "listen to people, see how they stick themselves into the world, hand them along a ways in their dark journey and be handed along, and for good and selfish reasons. It only remains to decide whether this vocation is best pursued in a service station or—." [14] We know that Binx Bolling decides on medical school, not a service station.

Closing Reflection

During an important change in my own life, and shortly after Walker Percy's death, I met with Robert Coles in his office at Adams House in Cambridge. Our three-hour discussion remains memorable. We spent most of that time talking about Walker Percy, his work, and Dr. Coles's friendship with Dr. Percy. I was touched by Dr. Coles's story of their friendship. His love and respect were obvious.

That day, we shared our reflections and concerns about education, about literature, about the moral and spiritual life. One of the many questions we discussed that spring day: Why literature? And why literature in medicine? Dr. Coles talked of his experiences teaching in medical institutions. He reflected on the fact that the humanities are considered "soft" and peripheral in medical education, in spite of the long history of esteemed and brilliant leaders in medicine who have argued for the ideally educated physician. Although medical ethics is considered necessary in the curriculum of most medical schools, the humanities remain not only "soft" but for the most part invisible.

Dr. Coles laughed when he told me of his experience at Harvard University, where individuals in the "hard" disciplines call his discussion of stories and narrative with students and residents a form of group therapy. He had a certain sadness in his eye when he asked rhetorically, "Why is reading and talking about feelings, about the human spirit, of what it is like to encounter another human being, why is this considered 'soft' and of secondary importance in what we do and think about in medicine?" Robert Coles envisions an educational environment where science, moral and spiritual reflection, and service to others sit side by side, all important in the training and work of future physicians.

Walker Percy helped me with such a vision. In this essay, I have tried to illustrate the thoughts and actions of one doctor-teacher concerned with the education of students not yet removed from their desire to help and understand the life and mind of others, and of interns, residents, and practitioners who have lost their way. Walker Percy's life and works can remind us of a practice of medicine that seeks meaning in the ordeal of suffering and pain, sees professional life and involvement with others in fresh and unique ways, and recovers the aspirations and ideals that sustain us when we are most in need of vision.

Notes

1 Jay Tolson, *Pilgrim in the Ruins* (New York: Simon and Schuster, 1992).

2 Robert Coles, *Walker Percy: An American Search* (Boston and Toronto: Little, Brown, 1978).

3 Walker Percy, "Diagnosing the Modern Malaise," in *Signposts in a Strange Land,* ed. Patrick Samway (New York: Farrar, Straus, and Giroux, 1991), 217.

4 Walker Percy, "From Facts to Fiction," in *Signposts in a Strange Land,* 188.

5 Walker Percy, "Physician as Novelist," in *Signposts in a Strange Land,* 193.

6 Percy, "From Facts to Fiction," 188.

7 Arthur Frank, *At the Will of the Body: Reflections on Illness* (Boston: Houghton Mifflin, 1991).

8 Anatole Broyard, *Intoxicated by My Illness* (New York: Fawcett Columbine, 1992), 44.

9 Arthur Frank, *The Wounded Storyteller: Body, Illness, and Ethics* (Chicago: University of Chicago Press, 1995), 15–16.

10 Frank, *The Wounded Storyteller,* 72.

11 Lionel Trilling, *The Liberal Imagination* (New York and London: Harcourt Brace Jovanovich, 1978).

12 Walker Percy, "The Loss of the Creature," in *The Message in the Bottle* (New York: Farrar, Straus, and Giroux, 1978).

13 Walker Percy, *The Moviegoer* (New York: Ivy Books, 1990), 126.

14 Ibid., 204.

Now You Are One of Us:

Gender, Reversal, and the Good Read

Laurie Zoloth

The Skin of the Hero

I like to talk to strangers, having a California upbringing, so I am happy on buses. One time, on one of those little airport shuttles in which several passengers from a general direction are picked up at the curb and taken home, I happen onto the best of instant American discourse, the kind that occurs in situations of slight catastrophe. We have been promised much that we know will not come true, swiftness and clarity of direction, but I do not mind. The bus driver is a Russian, and we take turns telling him the way to our neighborhoods. It takes a long time. The man on my seat and I pass the time with talk about reading the Bible. Like me, he is a graduate student, a priest sent off by the Jesuits to study systematic theology and to meet the Jews and the Buddhists and the Baptists. We talk about the feeling of reading along in, say, Genesis, and wanting the story to come out differently, reading ourselves into the text, the being-thereness of the tale, the heat of the desert, Abraham in the dark black tent, hearing the bells on the camels of the travelers as they come toward him, waiting on his thick red rug. My Jesuit seat mate is quiet. Ducking his head down in the dark, not to offend, he says, how it can possibly be that I can read the Bible like that? Don't I notice, he asks, kindly, that it is not addressed to me? A woman? That the "you" of the tale, the subject, is, well, a guy?

To be frank, I don't, which is to say, yes, if I think about it, but not usually, any more than I think about it in Plato, or Hume, or *Merck's Manual.* The totality of the address and the totality of the gaze envelope me, and I become the hero in the story, and the one to whom it is written, the good citizen, the Israelite searching the sky for the column of fire to follow, the solemn Greek householder, the doctor searching the patient for the clue. And in the good read, the read that is the struggle for the good act, the reading of the moral life, I carry the whole matter of the self internally, wearing the skin of my woman-self, but holding the choices, which is to say, the choosing male self, inside. I realize that when I read, I read like a woman who is reading like a man, doubling the text, a woman pregnant with sons.

This is the instantiational process of reading itself and why the act of reading is a moral event, a recognition, and an encounter that will change both the reader and the text, and rewrite the story that the reader will tell to the next. And so it is with all moral gestures, and why the moral act of medicine, the reading of the text of the body and the heart of the other, the highest stakes read of all, rests on the possibility of becoming the other, of the reversal and the doubling that all moral life demands: now I am you, seeing the world with these eyes, and now you are one of us.

This last phrase comes from the extraordinary writer-physician Walker Percy, the subject of this volume about reading and medicine and being a patient. Percy, in his life and his fiction, allows us an intimate entrance into the very moment in which the reversal is powerfully enacted, the moment in which the powerful physician (or hero as researcher, healer, knower of truth) has turned to face himself as a patient, dis-eased, crazy as a loon, and is just as instinctively coming on home through an unfamiliar sky. Percy's search—and the read on which he invites us, in the middle of the life we will watch as he watches it—is the search for the good act, for the good home in the world of falsity, easy happiness, and banal duplicity.

From such a gifted writer one expects much, and as the others in this volume gracefully testify, Percy is perhaps the modern American writer who well meets this expectation. But what is happening, as my Jesuit friend might ask, when one reads Percy from the perspective of a woman, and a Jew? Don't I notice that the text is not addressed to me? That I am object and not subject? That Jews stand for the exiled self, and women and nature for the escape? It is, of course, this noticing and this complexity that I want to explore in this essay, an essay that is not the easy complaint (literature is about difference, after all; Percy is Percy, not Angelou) but an essay that notices that women characters in the wonderful novels emerge at the end, however they begin, as solutions to despair rather than as actors against it.

This does not have to be the case in thinking about existential dis-ease, and in fact, Percy's contemporaries Sylvia Plath and Anne Sexton, women writers who also struggled with despair, offer telling insights about the problem from within the woman's epistemic stance. The very domesticity that Percy portrays as salvific, Sexton and Plath reveal as dangerous.

When reading Percy, then, the reversal, the act of imagining ourselves into the periphery, and out of the margins into the center, becomes the heart of the work, a circle that tells us much about the distances we have come, like the repetitions that Percy's characters enact in his novels.

Women and the Weather

The researcher is the one who "looks again," and the men who are at the center of Percy's work are, above all, careful observers of the world, on both a search and a research project. Like all really decent physicians, they understand that they are also on a search for themselves, for the good path through the chaos of illness and loss. For example, Will Barrett, the hero in *The Second Coming,* looks for the clinical evidence of God's existence with the dedication and the method of the scientist in a clinical trial. "His plan was simple: wait. The elegance of it pleased him. As cheerfully as a puttering scientist who hits on a simple elegant experiment which will, must, must, yield a clear yes or no, he set about his calculations. The trick was to devise a single wait which would force one of two answers, not more, not less."[1]

Will Barrett (who will both bear it and bare it, finally, his tragedy and his loss) is the perfect Percyean hero. First we are made to understand that this fictive hero is not only male, he is the hypermale of southern legend; he is Rhett Butler with irony: rich, handsome, widely able, the very best at whatever he does, subtle, sensual and sexual, and very fit. He will have acquired awards and honors, and the best stuff. But none of it will matter.[2] In fact, we will learn much of what is admirable about our guy from the admiring comments of others, since the truly heroic man is not a braggart. In contrast to the finely observed bones and tendons and follicles of the women we meet, we are given the barest of details of the body of the hero.

In *The Moviegoer,* Binx Bolling, the hero, medical student to be, is also on a scientific mission, a search. He awakes "like a castaway on a desert island" intent on understanding his remove from the crushing everydayness of life and proceeds on "the search. . . . He pokes around the neighborhood and he doesn't miss a trick."

These are men who are skilled at the games of men: fast sports cars, golf, and guns, especially guns. They are never brutal—brutality is a mark of the enemies in the stories—but they are very, very good shots. They understand and are easy with the weather and moods of the landscape, gazing at the world with the careful, sustained attention of a scientist. The object of the gaze, the poking, is the natural world. And in that world, achingly beautiful, the sky icing over with light, the leaves transcendent with the light, the sweet southern fields lit with the perfection of sunrise, women—good women, that is—are seen as another terrain, the curve of the cheek, the fall of hair, a terrain that can be known. Women are a kind of weather, or a kind of unknown territory for Percy, loved, when they are loved, for their loveliness, the order of a settled landscape, but dismissed for falsity, and for ugliness.

Percy's women are of two genres. The first is the kind of woman that the hero desires: she is just lovely, sensual, a woman to be kissed, with not a thought in her head, except perhaps of him; and these women, when they are good, are not only erotic but oddly efficient—good nurses, good secretaries, they will take good care of our hero. These are the women who will easily sleep with him.

The second type are the fellow travelers. And here Percy's poignant genius is at its very best. In his two best portrayals of women who are also caught up in "the search," we have a complex, insightful, and memorable portrayal of women and despair. These are beautiful, passionate, tough, strong, and very smart women, like the hero; they are smart, and they know the business at hand. Because they are women and not men, although they are described as "twins" to the existential hero travelers, their craziness is the central problem of the beginning of the narrative. Unlike the men, the women cannot hide behind competent roles. They have been named as nuts, and they have been captured as patients in the clinical world; they are the subjects—unlike the deeply suicidal men—of suicide watches, electroshock, lithium. Yet in both of Percy's finest works, in which two wonderful women are depicted and their internal narratives finely drawn, this complex portrayal lasts only for a while. By the end of the book, both women have been diminished, domesticated and rendered voiceless, or rather, given the broken hesitant voices of girl children, and given the aspirations of housewives. It is a heartbreakingly near miss.

Arms like a Man

How does such a transformation happen, and what is the meaning of this for the reader? And can we gain anything by the insight that what Percy does as a writer is precisely what often happens in the medical encounter, within the relationship between doctor (gendered male) and patient (gendered female)?

Perhaps the best rendition of the internal experience of the narrow ridge between madness and insightful analytic thought begins in the chapters of Percy's *The Second Coming.* Here we meet Allie, who has just walked herself out of a mental hospital by successfully executing an elaborate and carefully planned escape. Her struggle, we learn, is a struggle not with feelings of unhappiness but with the code of language itself, a complex and elegant insistence on hearing and speaking the actual true thing in conversation. Her struggle for actual meaning, for careful consideration of the real behind the social, marks her (but only for us, the readers, in on it) not as nutty but as beautifully and wonderfully aware. The Allie we come to know through her letters to herself is literate, lyrical, and a good writer, smart and trustworthy, in fact, the only sober and trustworthy person in the narrative so far, and the only one that the externally presented "Allie" can count on.

Her first acts mark her and regender her. She cuts her hair short so that she looks like, and indeed is mistaken for, a boy. She buys army surplus clothes, a furthering of the male disguise, and loves the pleasure of big hiking boots. If a female psychiatric patient is presented as a caricature of a woman (in a housedress, in slippers, hysterical-trouble-in-the-womb, unable to work, weak), then Allie's new life will be a rebuttal of all that. The world presented to her as a good southern woman has been a world of lies, illusion, and emptiness. The Allie reborn as boy is unwilling to speak at all unless she uses the most literal, most examined of language.

Allie's second coming, her redemption, it first seems to us, is to come into the power of the analytic discerning self that is the author of the letters and the interior observer of a world that is deeply flawed. She hikes into the lost greenhouse, the Edenic world of nature, and there enacts the Adamic tasks (not the Eve ones): she meets an animal and names it into love, hauls wood and builds fires, learns to hitch up and haul things that are far heavier than her own woman's weight in the world. Our girl, or rather our boy, is doing just fine.

But the ostensive hero of the tale is not the carefully observed Allie but the paragon Will Barrett, who despite having "gone as far as he could go" and having not just wealth and power but the very most wealth and power and prestige possible in his world, is lost in a crisis of meaning more potent than Allie's. On the other side of the golf course, in a world tamed utterly by modernity, under the watch of a faith tamed utterly by modernity, Will searches for God. But unlike Allie, who is looking for light, warmth, and food, a way to "walk correctly," Will (by, of course, an act of will) is looking for death, seeking in the re-membering and reenacting of his father's death the truth that he yearns for. What Will comes to remember is the central event in his own childhood, long repressed, that his father, on understanding that his son Will "was one of us, now"—meaning one of the depressed, lost men of his family—believes he would be better off dead. The father tries to kill him and himself, but does not succeed at either.

Will, too, sheds the skin of clothes, success, house, and stuff, to come to the darkness of the woods, to test God in the womb of the world, an ancient cave just adjacent to the greenhouse, light and air that Allie has made. It is at this juncture that Will's redemption is made possible, but by an Allie who has turned her attention toward the restoration of a nineteenth-century oven and stove. It is the symbol of a lost past, and of a world in which a woman is lit not by the passion for true language, for clarity in writing, but by the home fire. She will describe the careful cleaning of the stove and then, having hauled it improbably into the center of the greenhouse, will buy meat and cook it for Will.

Will fails at his suicide attempt, is so lost, fallen so profoundly, that he has lost language itself. He literally falls into her greenhouse, and Allie, with competence and certainly will, redeems him. She turns her attention and energy finally toward caring for Will, "picking him up" when he falls, washing him "like a nurse of comatose people," and imagines herself as that nurse. "She did not mind bathing a man. How nice people were, unconscious! They do not glance. Yes, she should be a nurse of unconscious patients. Again, it was a matter of calculating weights and angles and hefts. The peculiar recalcitrant slack weight of the human body required its own physics. . . . Exhausted, she cooked a supper of oatmeal and made a salad of brook lettuce and small tart apples."[3]

In *The Moviegoer,* the brilliant but mad hero also completely "falls" and is hoisted to his feet by the resources and power of the woman who shares his insight, intellect, and madness. Like Allie, Kate—cousin, confidant, and fellow traveler—has a thin, boyish body and wears boy's clothes, "shirts and jeans." We meet her as she is working in the basement, restoring lost ironwork. Kate is the only one in the novel who understands that Jack (Binx) Bolling is in the grip of a deep and profound existential crisis. "You are as crazy as I am, Jack." They discuss the "search" that Binx is engaged in. "And the danger is of becoming no one nowhere. . . . Kate parses it out with the keen male bent of her mind yet with her women's despair. Therefore I take care to be no more serious than she."[4]

If Allie masters the natural world that nearly defeats Will, Kate (the counterpart to Binx) masters the urban Chicago "genie-soul" that has paralyzed him. While he is in the terrified grip of "rays" shooting out from strangers in the street, Kate is making travel arrangements, reading maps, taking charge of the money: "I had never noticed how shrewd and parsimonious she was."[5] Indeed, "Kate looks after me. . . . Kate takes charge with many a cluck and much fuss, as if she had caught sight of me in a howling void and meant to conceal it from the world. All of a sudden she is a regular city girl."[6]

In *Love in the Ruins,* the pattern varies only slightly, but it is Ellen, the tough woman who can carry the gun, who loves her work as a nurse, who "spits on my eyebrows and smooths them," who is constantly picking up the hero Tom and setting him "straight," who ends up as his good wife. Unlike Tom's first wife, who "hates the ordinary," the Ellen we meet at the end of the book suddenly loves nothing more than cooking and cooking for her husband. In the last chapter, Ellen will not leave the stove except for the bed.

The act of salvation and power is a brief epiphany, and it is quickly lost. The women whom the reader might come to see as being on a similar—indeed a twinned—journey of insight and irony, a journey that seeks above all for meaning, for love, and for the truth in language, suddenly want nothing more than to be taken to bed and transformed by love.

And in this process, in which Will is founded, cleansed, redeemed, and healed (by a woman young enough to be his daughter), and in which Binx is reoriented, we see Allie lose her interior voice entirely; we see Kate return from Chicago as the docile bride. They sleep with the hero, and for the women we have come to see as the stronger of the doubled hero, that seems to do the trick. Says Allie: "It is now evident that whatever was wrong with me is now largely cured. Quel mystery." She becomes, in the text, the simple beautiful lover, and she will be the good wife; there will be "two children, a girl and a boy," whom she will walk to school. She will do what she is told and speak only to us now in the simple sentences of the external Allie. They will have the children, a girl and a boy just like the ones that we will see in *Love in the Ruins,* neatly asleep, and perfect, possessions.

Raising the Fallen

The women who become men, with strong arms ("the lean muscular and sturdy bodies") and no pretense, who are writers and searchers, end up as child-wives. In *The Second Coming* and in *The Moviegoer,* we see the narrative potency of the women, who are also mad, who are "one of us," shaped like a boy and thinking "in a male way," who end up asking "to be told just what to do" each step, in simple sentences. In short, they are seen as nurses, in the terms of a classic physician relationship, good, caring, but needing orders.

Here is that moment in *The Second Coming:* "What pleasure, obeying instructions! . . . She clapped her hands for joy. What a discovery! To get a job, to do it well, which is a pleasure, please the employer [remember here that the one who is ordering her is her lover, Will]. . . . That was the secret! All this time she had made a mistake. She had thought (and her mother had expected) that she must do something extraordinary."

And here it is again in *The Moviegoer:* "I think I see a way. It seems to me that if we were together a great deal and you tell me the simplest things and not laugh at me—I beg you for pity's own sake never to laugh at me—tell me things like: Kate, it is all right for you to go down to the drugstore, and give me a kiss, then I will believe you."[7]

And in *Love in the Ruins:* "Through the open doorway I can see Ellen standing at the stove in a patch of sunlight. She stirs grits. Light and air flow around her arm like the arm of Velazquez's weaver girl. Her apron is lashed just above the slight swell of her abdomen. She socks spoon down on pot and cocks her head to listen for the children. . . .Meg and Thomas More, Jr., are still asleep."[8]

So the woman reader loses, or is left, or must finally go on, but as the male hero, since it will be he who ends up with the life world that Percy urges us to know as redemption, a second chance. All the men do, in fact, end up as decent professionals, not big shots but country lawyer (Will), country doctor (Tom), and quietly achieving medical student (Binx). Women end up with no job except wife and hence ultimately function as part of the solution rather than as codefendant, coconspirator, or coresearcher, as they begin. If simplicity and domesticity are the answer to existential searches, then what is found is the idealized beauty of the daily, which will exist for our heroes in a world far different from the real politic of the first marriages, in which children die (brothers, daughters), women age and become ugly and fat, or women yearn for a life world or faith.

Dis-ease, discomfiture with the routinized, bourgeois superficiality of the era, the dumbness of that happiness generated by golf and country clubs and piety is not unique to Percy. His insight that the perception is a part of the task of the outsider, and the necessity for restoration, is the constant frame of his novels. Women who get this are like men, which genders the illness as male, which calls for a male answer for the reader, an answer in which women are structurally needed to play a structured role: a person to come home to.

Meanwhile, Back at the Ranch

Yet it is at this very moment, in the redeemed, lovely, simple home, that much of women's literature on depression and meaning begins. To read the work of the women writers who are contemporaries of Percy is to read the terror-tale of Allie all grown up, after the "two lovely children" are taken off to school and the good wife returns home, or after the cooking is done and the beautiful stove is all clean. For readers of Sylvia Plath and Anne Sexton (the two women most strongly identified with the depiction of illness), it will be impossible to read of a woman who has been mentally ill, alone with her sleeping children and her stove, without an awareness of the text beneath the text: like Plath and Sexton, she just might kill herself in the nice warm gas.[9]

Sexton and Plath, like Percy, write to us about the oddity of the doubled role of the patient who is the observer, the poet who is looking for the precise meaning of the language that other people use so casually. Percy attends in a hospital as a medical intern, and he catches a disease, tuberculosis, that will make him a patient; but it will be his insight as a patient, as others in this book have noted, that will allow him to find his voice as a writer. Sexton is a housewife who becomes "depressed" by the act of mothering. She is admitted to a mental institute and is able to emerge from her despair only by the act of examination, a reversal. She reads medical and psychiatric textbooks. She tells friends, "Someone asked me the other day if my doctor is analytical, I said, 'No—just me!' "[10]

Sexton cannot escape, but by understanding her illness, she becomes the confessed confessor to others who struggle with depression. Both a persona and a search for a self inhabit her work. She understands the thinness of the line between the patient's insight and the patient's illness; she struggles with the problem of whether the medication that she must take to preserve her life will destroy her art, which is the perceptive, ironic, truthful, and insightful search beneath the surface of modernity, "happiness," and suburban life.

Will the medication allow for clarity or destroy the hero's ability to act passionately? Percy suggests that the diagnosis of madness is an error, that senility and confusion come from the lack of good work, or careful attention, or ignorance. Percy writes us young children who are wise and thoughtful, far better conversation partners than adults. But Sexton knows trouble when she sees it. She is unable to mother her own daughters, and she cannot cook or clean or make a home—she sits in a corner of the dining room, surrounded by piles of poems and books and the noise of everyone, and she writes the poems that will win her the Pulitzer Prize. But it is the yearning to be the good wife that will elude her. She will ask her husband to stroke her hair every night and tell her, "You are a good girl, Anne." But she is not: to be a good girl is beyond her. And when a woman fails to keep house, it is only through illness that this is allowed. Percy can write in bed for hours before he leaves his room, but Sexton cannot do this until she breaks her hip or admits herself to the mental hospital. And like the women who are the seekers in Percy's novels, when a woman cannot function as a good girl, she cannot hide this well, she will be marked as mad, and she will be a patient.

For this search, Sexton will tell us, children and home are no answer. Despite wanting children deeply, they are difficult and, for these women writers, a distraction that is real, however beloved.

Sexton understands the difference between how the male and the female writer come to understand their work. She writes the following poem to her lover, the poet James Wright:

The Black Art

A woman who writes feels too much,
those trances and portents!
As if cycles and children and islands
weren't enough; as if mourners and gossips
and vegetables were never enough.
She thinks she can warn the stars.
A writer is essentially a spy.
Dear love, I am that girl.

A man who writes knows too much,
such spells and fetishes
As if erections and congresses and products
weren't enough; as if machines and galleons
and wars were never enough.
With used furniture he makes a tree.
A writer is essentially a crook.
Dear love, you are that man.[11]

Unlike Percy's, Sexton's solution is not to be found in the simple pleasures of the domestic—even there, with writers (seers) there is going to be trouble. Children and cooking will not fix the "never enoughness"; domesticity "will not warn stars." The poem continues:

Never loving ourselves,
hating even our shoes and our hats,
we love each other, precious, precious
Our hands are light blue and gentle.
Our eyes are full of terrible confessions.
But when we marry,
the children leave in disgust.
There is too much food and no one left over
to eat up all the weird abundance.[12]

In this poem, one can see vividly the "male intellect with the women's emotions" that Percy's male character Binx Bolling avoids, and that Percy, as writer, domesticates. Sexton is not alone. Sylvia Plath also explores the problem of being at the same moment, the woman who is a mental patient struggling with depression and the writer who is a seer of the truth of the broken world, the teller of the realest tale of all. Plath strains like Sexton to live in a world described by Percy as ideal, telling Sexton in a letter about beekeeping, baking, having babies, and writing, too. But love, marriage, and babies just won't do it for Plath, either. There is something difficult and actual in the demand made even by the sleeping baby. Compare this excerpt from Plath's poem "Morning Song" to Percy's description of Tom Moore waking to his sleeping babies:

> All night your moth-breath
> Flickers among the flat pink rose. I wake to listen:
> A far sea moves in my ear.
>
> One cry, and I stumble from bed, cow-heavy and floral
> In my Victorian nightgown.
> Your mouth opens clean as a cat's. The window square
>
> Whitens and swallows its dull stars . . . [13]

Here the stars are not warned; they are dulled and consumed by the same needy hunger as that of the child, the lyric sea far, and the coming of morning, meaning the coming of work, of mothering. As with Sexton and the Allie we meet in her letters to herself, for Plath the trick of health is to convince the doctors that you are again on their side: to be sane, not-patient, is to have the perceptions of the physician, to learn to "see" things their way. Consider Plath's fictionalized account of her emergence from her hospital admission: "There ought, I thought, to be a ritual for being born twice— patched, retreaded and approved for the road, I was trying to think of one when Doctor Nolan appeared from nowhere and touched me on the shoulder. . . . The eyes all turned themselves toward me, and guiding myself by them, I stepped into the room." [14]

It is not only the personae of the women writers who can tell us of the cost of a woman's despair and a male sensibility, of the price when the hero who is a seeker is also a wife, or of what it means to yearn for stars and galaxies at the stove, cooking, in the whitening world, as the sea becomes inaudible. In fact, the very physician most respected as the chronicler and researcher of depression and mania, Kay Redfield Jamison, describes this issue in a book in which she confesses that she, too, is a manic-depressive, not merely a scientist who writes about "them."

Jamison recalls her first visit to a mental ward, as, of course, an observer. "Although fascinated, I was primarily frightened by the strangeness of the patients. . . . even stronger than the terror, however was the expression of pain in the eyes of the women. . . . Some part of me instinctively reached out and in an odd way understood this pain, never imagining that I would someday look in the mirror and see their sadness and insanity in my own eyes."[15]

Jamison comes to see her madness deepen, and although it offers her "extraordinary, shattering and shifting light, inconstant but ravishing colors laid out across miles of circling rings," she understands that only medication, therapy, and a turning away from the disquiet of her illness will allow her to use her gifts. Because she is a scientist, and ultimately can live on the physician side of the divide as a faculty member at Johns Hopkins Medical School, she re-creates a life world in which the search is not abandoned, not romanticized, not denied, and not sublimated into the home: in short, she comes up with the male, not the female, solution to depression.

In crossing over the line into patienthood from physicianhood, a line carefully guarded in medical training, in what Jamison describes as the role reversal of therapy, we have something very like the experience that Percy and Sexton can create for us as readers. We are inside the madness, and it seems a lot better on the whole in Percy's account than the world of sanity and dumbness from which the sleeper awakes. Aha, but Jamison reminds us, and finally as the real-life deaths of Sexton and Plath painfully record, it is not so simple. In real life, mental illness just might be fatal; the stroke victim cannot snap out of hemiplegia with an act of will.

The Physician-Patient Relationship:
Cross-Dressing in White

So if we can be offered this sober account of the "truthful" journey, why read fiction about madness at all, and if the reading self is a woman, why read a writer in which the imagined reader is not a woman at all, but (as I imagine it) a hunting buddy?

Martha Nussbaum, in her account of why we read about love and the moral life in philosophy and fiction, reminds us that authorship is a complex authority. She describes three figures among which we must distinguish: "1) the narrator or the author-character (together with this character's conceptions of the reader); 2) the authorial presence that animates the text taken as a whole (together with the corresponding implicit picture of what a sensitive and informed reader will experience); and 3) the whole of the real-life author and reader, much of which has no causal relations to the text and no relevance to the proper reading of the text." [16]

Reading is the act of discovery of the world that is just beyond, the world in which the reader is on to the complex activity of searching and understanding. [17] Nussbaum's intricate point is that the moral activity of a philosophical search for a good life, for the moral ways to live, is found in the forms of fiction in which the form matters. I would agree and add that it is not the form alone, but the process, the work, which is to say the conversational encounter that fiction demands, the trying on of possible clothes of alterity itself, that creates a place for the work of moral philosophy.

In the very reading of serious fiction like that which Percy is writing for us (for himself), the act of becoming the other serves as the act of seeing the other profoundly and complicatedly as one slips in and out of the embodied self that holds the text. I know that I am my own reader-self in the moments in which, for example, I come across a paragraph about the Jew: "Jews are my first real clue. When a man is in despair and does not in his heart of hearts allow that a search is possible and when such a man passes a Jew in the street, he notices nothing. . . . But when such a man awakens to the possibility of a search and when such a man passes a Jew in the street for the first time, he is like Robinson Crusoe seeing the footprint on the beach." [18]

Or when I come across a paragraph about a woman: "She's the girl of our dreams, Americans! The very one we held in our heart as we toiled in the jungles of Ecuador. She is! Sitting scrunched over and humpbacked, she is beautiful despite herself, calf yoga-swelled over heel, one elbow propped, the other winged out like a buzzard for all she cares." [19]

But if I keep reading, I enter again the skin of the reader-self that is called out by the text itself, the reader that the author will need me to be for my journey to go on, and ultimately for the textual journey to go on as well. The reading is both disrupted by the attention to the being of the reader and subverted in a very interesting way for the reader who is also interested in how the read teaches us something about medicine. To read as a Percy reader is to read an act of transgression, not only his transgression and insight into the role of patient and illness, but mine into the world of guns and power and science and certainty. This is a recapitulation of the journey of any medical professional—Jamison calls this the deeply, nearly exclusively male "club" of the profession. For a woman physician must do with her body—put on the white cloak of medicine, learn the language and the affections of the hunter, the researcher, the "male bent of mind," the roles read as male ones—what the woman reader of Percy must do with her reading. For the feminist who is a man, then the doubling is a double cross: to read like a girl means to read like a girl who is reading like a boy, crossing the boundaries, meaning that each awareness intensifies the experience of thinking, hard, about the meaning of boundaries themselves.

Encountering the other and making a relationship in the space, the clear air that surrounds you, is the work of ethics; and encountering the other in the clinic and making meaning of the work of healing and being healed is the work of bioethics—or at least it begins the language of bioethics when we speak of this work. Reading fiction is the recapitulation of this kind of conversation, or it is the imagining of how it might be, or what it might be. One can wear the white coat of the physician, the white gown of the patient, or the white cloak of the writer who is "spy," who is "crook." One can learn secrets and the art of decency.

Reading as Percy, one can read both as a physician and as a patient. Reading as a reader who is one of us, one can feel, as in the words of Carl Elliott, that this is written just for me, and also feel the transgression: I am inside and I am outsider, subject and object of the gaze. The paradox is that "knowing" in literature offers hope that the condition is both shared and possible to transcend, word by word.

Reading, for Goodness' Sake

But I as a reader am not just any old sort, either. Does it matter to you, reader of the reader's tale of reading who I am, what I might strangely confess? Would this compromise my scholarship, would you trust me less? Can I write about depressed men, and searches and whether medication is redemptive or a defeat? For each of us who reads, and reads for goodness' sake, is as lost as Percy's—Binx Bolling's—Crusoe on the desert island, and each who reads and teaches the text of illness and medicine is glancing at a held mirror. Percy's women care for Percy's men; the hero cannot leave the mess that he is in alone, never does; he needs a woman he can trust on the journey, and in some way, we all, as readers of fiction for better (as in Percy) or for worse (as in Sexton), become the woman you can trust, there on the road.

As Nussbaum knows about the writer, so the reader has some work of discernment as well: here is your life, and here is the life of the author, and here is the life of the persona of the author, and here is the fictional self that we will dream about and argue with. There is the reader that I am: woman who imagines herself a man, Jew, ethicist; and there is the reader that Percy, or Plato, imagines for himself.

Here is what I have come to the text with, what I have been dis-tracked-ted by as I write: depression is like riding a bicycle, a stance once acquired that becomes instantly familiar, a place in the body that the body will remember. This spring, my dark-eyed son learned to do both. I watched from just behind as he caught his balance and as he woke to the sorrow and the unfairness of the world and it made him angry and sad. He is very good at both, learning the bicycle in one day, and he is "in it," the sorrow of things, as Percy would say. He wakes hungry, yearning. Like his father, my son wakes up close to tears, and I cannot fix either one. He is one of us, has noticed something is wrong, and he will not be easily bought off.

We take him to the doctor, the chief doctor, too. He has us fill out forms that will document his father's anger, his father's parent's rages. Unlike Percy, his father cannot trace the line of furious men for generations, since for most American Jews, all the family beyond this has been obliterated in a lost Europe. But the doctor looks at the form, sees my boy for ten minutes, and is ready to sign him right up in his therapeutic trials of a powerful new drug, one that will make my boy happy, one that it just so happens the doctor is in the middle of trying out (though not in a clinical trial), and he shows me the article he has published that proves it is so. He is a very famous physician. He looks at me and tells me that he has decided what my boy has is maternally transmitted on my genotype, and that I, too, must have a family rocked by anger and despair. I imagine generations and continents of my lost family, exiled, pursued, furious. We are the Jews, marked as outsiders; we are offering the first clues.

It takes me, a bioethicist and a feminist, a few days and a few good friends, other doctors, to sort this one out. We don't give him the drugs. Instead, I try the Percy response: we go to the beach, we hang about with him. And this seems to help. I feed him, like a Percymother, I teach him to swim in hard and large waves. For an hour, we play cat's cradle with an old piece of string; it is a game with no ending, I tell him, so let's see what we've got. I tell him that I know the world is not fair, that learning to read will help him a lot, and then, word by word by word, I sit with him and I show him what I know about that.

Notes

1 Walker Percy, *The Second Coming* (New York: Simon and Schuster, 1980), 244.

2 Although money and position do not matter, one still cannot imagine the doctors, lawyers, and heirs as day laborers.

3 *The Second Coming,* 270.

4 Walker Percy, *The Moviegoer* (New York: Avon, 1960), 270.

5 Ibid., 70.

6 Ibid., 164.

7 Ibid., 161.

8 Walker Percy, *Love in the Ruins* (New York: Ballantine Books, 1989), 325.

9 It is, of course, the subject of yet another work to see also how the use of the word and symbol "oven" works in any post-Holocaust text. For the Holocaust, and its oven, constantly reappear for Percy. Jews operate as the stand-in for exile, for the deepest loss, and, in Percy's understanding, painfully and unknowing of the facts, for blindness and acquiescence in the face of evil. Suffice it to say here that Jews are also, like Percy, exiles, outsiders, perceivers of the truth, until they are not. The ultimate betrayal of the Jews for Percy is when they "become like everyone else." In *The Second Coming,* the real Jews disappoint; we hear of their sexual depravity, their refusal of real faith, their refusal of their role in history. To count on the Jews becomes the symptom of real (meaning treatable, chemical) craziness.

10 Diane Middlebrook, *Anne Sexton: A Biography* (Boston: Houghton Mifflin, 1991).

11 Anne Sexton, "The Black Art," in *The Poetry Anthology: 1912–1977,* ed. Darly Hine and Joseph Parini (Boston: Houghton Mifflin, 1978), 386.

12 Ibid.

13 Sylvia Plath, "Morning Song," in *The Columbia Anthology of American Poetry,* ed. Jay Parini (New York: Columbia University Press, 1995), 675.

14 Sylvia Plath, *The Bell Jar* (New York: Harper and Row, 1971), 275.

15 Kay Redfield Jamison, *An Unquiet Mind: A Memoir of Moods and Madness* (New York: Alfred. A Knopf, 1995).

16 Martha Nussbaum, *Love's Knowledge: Essays on Philosophy and Literature* (New York: Oxford University Press, 1990).

17 Ibid., 6.

18 *The Moviegoer,* 75.

19 *Love in the Ruins,* 297.

Inherited Depression, Medicine, and Illness in Walker Percy's Art

Bertram Wyatt-Brown

Nothing makes us greater than a great suffering.—Alfred de Musset

When genius takes hold of us, we are full of audacity, yea almost mad and heedless of health, life, and honor. . . . [But] let genius once leave us . . . we feel as if we were in the midst of shelterless rocks with the tempest raging about us.—Nietzsche

Walker Percy had a lifelong preoccupation with his family's history of depression and with medicine, his first choice of profession. His writing also explored his personal tendency to melancholy and proneness to physical ailment that began with a siege of tuberculosis in his early adulthood. In his writings he translated these concerns into his diagnosis of "sickness unto death" in modern society. To overcome the circumstances he proposed the need for human connection not only with God but with the past, especially the familial past. At the same time he dealt with the role of medicine, its blessings and its curse. He recognized the elegance and promise of the field, but he also discerned its limitations, especially in handling psychological dilemmas. Yet his medical training provided him with a stabilizing element when problems of depression haunted him. Christian faith and absorbing interests in linguistics and philosophy helped him through such trials, but a proud sense of scientific professionalism was also significant. As Lewis Lawson notes, Percy continued to list himself in the *American Medical Dictionary* long after he had left practice.[1]

Nearly every novel that Walker Percy wrote featured doctors and their dilemmas in a way that suggests his intimate knowledge of what might be called the sociology of medicine, even though he early put down the pathologist's scalpel and took up the writer's pen. Below the surface, however, was an awareness of familial tragedy that required a persistent search for hope in the future—in this world as well as the next. These disparate but almost inseparable elements of science, genealogy, and illness came together to create the richness and complexity of his art.

First to be explored is the least well-known aspect of Percy's past, the history of the Percy line, with its remarkable record of high achievement in many fields, suicide, and early death. The subject demonstrates, too, that Percy was not the first in the lineage to ponder in fiction the meaning of the family condition and to do so in an imaginative manner not unlike his own. There follows a discussion of how the novelist's medical background intersected with that legacy and served as an anchor of certainty. Finally, an exploration of how his fiction evolved from personal to more universal concerns of all three issues—genetic melancholy, medicine, and illness, especially mental disorder—reveals the complex architecture of his creativity.

Before dealing with the question of inherited insanity and its place in Percy's art and life, something must be offered about the neurological phenomenon itself. It is important to understand what Walker Percy and his family had to confront at an earlier time when all known remedies proved ineffective. As it is now recognized, an imbalance of serotonin, dopamine, and other neurotransmitters may create the conditions for various forms of affective disorder. In some instances, chemical malfunctioning of a similar nature may be a significant factor in the frantic drive of the victim to kill all consciousness by suicide. As Edwin Schneidman, a leading expert on the topic, has observed, the act of self-destruction is "a multidimensional malaise in a heedful individual who defines an issue for which suicide is perceived as the best solution." The routines of eating, breathing, and working and all other functions no longer provide enjoyment or sense of purpose.[2] Walker Percy referred to this disillusionment with ordinary routine as "everydayness," a state of mind that he attributed to a perception of existential meaninglessness for so many souls in modern times.[3]

Everydayness, as it were, was particularly hard to bear in the era before the current array of drugs became available.[4] Nowadays, appropriate antidepressants, when calibrated in proper doses, along with psychotherapy and in rarer cases electroconvulsive therapy, offer at least partial relief that Walker Percy's forebears could not have received.[5] Molecular geneticists have uncovered some of the reasons why the illness persists in particular familial lines. In fact, the study of family histories, such as the Percys', assists in the process of scientific discovery. Investigations of twins, separated at an early age and placed in different environments, show a ratio of three times greater incidence of manic-depressive illness than that found in control groups (a concordance of 0.67 versus 0.20, respectively). Moreover, members of families with records of suicides deep in the past are far more at risk than the ordinary family would be. In a study of 243 patients with familial links to suicide, 48.6

percent had tried to kill themselves, most of them suffering from a form of affective disorder. Recent medical investigation shows that the risk factors of bipolar illness can be traced to chromosomal abnormalities.[6] Neurologists, geneticists, and biochemists have located some of the elements involved but are still working toward the disease's eradication.

Of course, the neurobiological elements can scarcely be proved beyond a doubt, at least not until genetics is more sophisticated than it is now. Nonetheless, reports in the national media indicate how fast medical advances have recently progressed toward an understanding of the brain's neural systems and mental disorders that arise from these systems' malfunctioning. Elliot S. Gershon, a leading expert at the National Institutes of Health, concludes that affective disorders such as the kind that Walker Percy's forebears, male or female, experienced "are familial, since the rate in relatives of patients is consistently about two or three times the rate in relatives of appropriately chosen case controls."[7] Rather than being the simple cause of the patient's anguish, however, these neurological factors might arise from the emotional effects of stress. As a result, somatic and psychic dysfunctions could be interconnected, even joined together.[8]

With regard to the first question of inherited depression, I draw on *The House of Percy*, my biography of the family. The Percys are an aristocratic, substantial breed of the Mississippi Delta. Yet as one of their neighbors observed in the 1930s, "tragedy pursues the Percy family like a nemesis."[9] For almost a hundred and fifty years, the family's members were struck down prematurely in life either by psychological or purely somatic maladies. For six generations of male Percys, the average age at death was thirty-nine (a lack of longevity that has since happily improved). Walker Percy, whom I met in 1987, was proud that he had outlasted all others on the family tree. The Percys' troubles were compounded by an additional, equally dismaying and irremediable problem that ordinarily but unjustly bears the stigma of moral weakness and condemnation. From 1794 to 1929, in each generation save one, a male member of the lineage took his own life, and women in the family had to be treated for madness. The first to take his own life was Charles Percy (1740–1794), who drowned himself in a tributary of the Mississippi River. Under such conditions of persistent tragedy, survivors cannot help but wonder what they contributed by action or neglect to such unhappy, even horrifying, situations.

In the generations nearest to the novelist's own era, the record was grievous. Walker Percy's paternal aunt Ellen Percy Murphy, great-aunt Lady Percy McKinney, and his great-great-uncle LeRoy Pope, who killed himself, suffered acutely from depression. His aunts had to be hospitalized for lengthy periods of their lives. Charles, the first Percy in America, had left Margaret, his Irish wife, still living in London when he disappeared to America about 1775. At age forty, he bigamously married a sixteen-year-old heiress and, with her dowry, established his growing family on cattle ranches and plantations in Spanish Mississippi and Louisiana. At the turn of the eighteenth century, his son by the unfortunate and lately deceased Margaret also moved into the same district. A predisposition to melancholy has appeared among Charles Percy's numerous descendants, particularly in the first American branch to which Walker Percy belonged.

Closer to the novelist himself, his uncle LeRoy Percy of Greenville, Mississippi, briefly a U.S. senator, knew the depths of sadness. According to his son William Alexander Percy, LeRoy could carouse like an Elizabethan but could also plunge into gloom while perspiration still dropped from his face; "you could feel him bleed inside." He could laugh and enjoy the good things of life, but never, Will Percy insisted, did he forget that human existence was "unbearably tragic."[10]

Still more drastically, Percy's father and his grandfather died by their own hands. Walker Percy (the novelist's grandfather), a wealthy Birmingham, Alabama, attorney, suffered a nervous collapse in 1911, received treatment at a hospital in Baltimore, and returned home allegedly cured. In the winter of 1917, however, he went upstairs in his house and fired a shotgun at his chest. His son LeRoy Pratt Percy had been waiting for his father in the library to plan a hunting expedition. Father and son were both avid sportsmen. Suffering from acute despair and sleeplessness, in 1925 LeRoy himself was admitted to the Johns Hopkins University Hospital. The authorities pronounced him cured after a few weeks under the then popular plan of somatic treatment that Emil Kraepelin had developed. (Freud's approach was not adopted at the Phipps Clinic until the early 1930s.)[11] Like his father a successful attorney in Birmingham, LeRoy Percy recovered for the time being. Yet the analyst George Zilboorg suggests that a son might fail to experience the normal pattern of grief and instead seek to "join" the dead father by following the same course that led to the parent's demise. We cannot know with certainty that this pattern occurred in the case of LeRoy Percy. In any event, twelve years after his own father's death, the novelist Walker Percy's father underwent another crisis of the mind that he did not choose to survive. LeRoy Percy killed himself in early June 1929, using his father's weapon of choice, a shotgun designed for sport. It was a method of suicide that appears in his son's novels, *The Last Gentleman* and *The Second Coming.*[12]

So unhappy a pattern of early death and melancholy was bound to affect Walker Percy's art and life in ways both overt and subtle. Speaking in the third person, he once claimed acquaintance with that "species of affliction which sets him apart and gives him an odd point of view. The wounded man has a better view of the battle than those still shooting." The writer, he continued, is less a prophet than a "canary that coal miners used to take down into the shaft to test the air." When the bird tweets his last note, "it may be time for the miners to surface and think things over."[13] Like Alfred de Musset, quoted in this essay's epigraph, Percy insisted that pain and inner ordeal had their indispensable uses. Yet the reaction to a father's suicide, especially for children, whose inexperience makes them vulnerable, could well lead to irremediable emotional damage. As Percy noted, his own role as a canary-like novelist showed how perilous the future was. Yet unlike the bird, he and fellow Percys did not expire at the first sign of trouble but showed enviable resilience and character under strain.

The second factor that helped to shape Percy's art was his fascination with the medical sciences, both somatic and psychiatric. Three factors led him along this path. They were a thirst for order and solidity, a reaction to his falling ill from tuberculosis, and his need, as he discovered, to deal with the curse of the Percy family. Percy's decision to become a physician had much to do with a reaction against the family's history. As a high-school and college student in the 1930s, following his father's suicide and his mother's accidental drowning in 1932, Percy seemed "more concerned with establishing absolute truths than with delving into complexities." So writes his biographer Jay Tolson. Percy was searching for "certainties" in a world that offered none.[14] His bout with tuberculosis also forced him into solitude, inactivity, and proximity to death—his own and those of others. At the two sanatoriums where he resided in the 1940s, he occupied himself with books of science, theology, philosophy, and fiction that probed the meaning of life and death. Thomas Mann, Franz Kafka, Fyodor Dostoyevsky, Søren Kierkegaard, Jacques Maritain, Gabriel Marcel, and other thinkers and novelists were sources for Percy's future literary experiments as well as instruments with which to probe his own mind. In particular, Dostoyevsky taught him that "suffering is an evil, yet at the same time through the ordeal of suffering one gets these strange benefits of lucidity, of seeing things afresh."[15] The melancholy temperament of the Russian intelligentsia, which Dostoyevsky shared in full measure, appealed to Percy. Moreover, like Percy himself, Dostoyevsky had lost his father during the son's teenage years by violence (murder). The two writers, Russian and American, grieved in anger and guilt but learned to cope through literary creativity and religious searching so that their sense of despair and suicidal rumination was assuaged.[16] Once, when depressed after completing a novel, Percy mused that his inner fury would eventually stimulate him as it had Dostoyevsky. "Malice, envy, pride, and other capital sins" could be the source of creativity itself, Percy wrote his friend Shelby Foote. "This, I am sure, was true in Dostoevsky's case; that he wrote best when simply angry, angry at a rather low level too, i.e. politically angry, ideologically angry etc." But how to translate that indignation at one's own or another's failure, weakness, and frustration into art? "If you are lucky and God loves you, you do the good things almost by inadvertence." But Percy worried that he could not match the artistry of Dostoyevsky and the other great masters. "Man," Percy once wrote in exasperation, "I can't write one of them saga-novels, wouldn't want to if I could, after Dostoevski and Tolstoy and Faulkner."[17]

Rather than deal, however, with Percy's literary resources and influences, we concentrate on his psychiatric interests and their origins. The novelist's attitude toward the family malady was much more complex than one might expect. Faced with the record of tragic losses among his relatives, Percy found it necessary as a young medical student at Columbia to seek therapeutic help. Over time, that decision brought together his medical, genetic, and literary concerns because the field of mental investigation was devoted to curing sickness of the soul, as it were, as well as of the body. Janet Rioch, his New York psychoanalyst from Canada, was developing a large practice. She had long been associated with fellow New York analysts Karen Horney, Erich Fromm, and Clara Thompson, and especially Harry Sullivan, a friend of Percy's guardian in Mississippi, William Alexander Percy.[18] For three years Percy underwent the rigors of prolonged therapy, five days a week. A female analyst might not have seemed the wisest choice for a proud young southerner steeped in conservative traditions about the sexual division. Yet Rioch's distance from the ways of the South could have been itself a great help in their mutual work.[19]

Percy's representation of the experience in Will Barrett's sessions with Dr. Gamow, a fashionable analyst in *The Last Gentleman*, may have come from this experience. If so, the expected transference and degree of openness it is supposed to engender were never completed. Will Barrett parries the doctor's inquiries with southern courtesy that, for the first year of treatment, "royally entertained" the analyst. During the second year of association, however, Gamow grows weary of his dance with a "Southern belle" of a partner, "light on his feet and giving nothing away." On the last visit after Will Barrett has bought his expensive telescope, Gamow gets the picture. "So now it seems you have spent your money on an instrument which will enable you to see the truth once and for all?" Barrett shrugs his shoulders and smiles. "It would be pretty nice," continues the doctor, "if we could find a short cut and get around all this hard work." Realizing that his patient is never going to cooperate, Gamow grows irritated and observes that Will Barrett has already had serious fugue states, is about to enter another, and always buys a costly object of pleasure, such as the telescope, before quitting analysis. Walker Percy knew very well the feints and means of repression that a patient might employ to hide painful truths of past experience. He also recognized that the rigid formulations of Freudian analysis of his day were not well designed to move the patient from passivity and obstruction to self-knowledge. Surely Gamow has learned from some source about the suicide of Will Barrett's father, a trauma to which the young engineer has never even alluded. If Gamow is ignorant of the facts, some delicate probing could certainly have elicited from Will Barrett a few clues on which to proceed. By exercising a certain passivity himself, however, the analyst has unwittingly colluded with his patient's unwillingness to lance the psychological boil, so to speak, and start anew.[20]

In this account, the novelist offers one of the best illustrations of how patient-analyst relations can become flawed. Although Percy's Will Barrett likes, even admires, the analyst, the hero has fashioned his "amiability" into a weapon of defense. Will Barrett secretly feels superior to the lisping doctor and silently mocks the fresh-faced, middle-class, "chicken-shit" Ohioans whom he meets in the group therapy sessions that Gamow has him join. The only clue to his inner life that the patient discloses is a confession of having a "hollowness" at the core of his being. Yet the cause of it never emerges in the years of treatment under Gamow's supervision. When Will Barrett terminates their relationship early in the story, he has still not learned who he really is.

Percy's astute rendering of an analytic experience that ends in failure does not, however, necessarily mirror exactly what occurred in his own life. Although experiencing the common difficulties of such an association, most probably he gained more insight into his own life than his character Will Barrett does. Although he never said so, Walker learned that some uncontrollable force would not inevitably carry him toward the same end that his father had met. At times, however, he may have worried that it might. As analyst Felix Brown has pointed out, the loss of a father is highly calamitous for a child, and the result is very often a strongly depressive reaction. Yet, Brown speculates, the mourning process may lead the orphan, if gifted, to develop his or her own resources and imagination. As "a virtue" arising from "necessity," deprivation could have remarkable results. So it was, anyhow, in Walker Percy's case.[21] Yet Percy himself only reluctantly admitted that the psychoanalytic experience had been worthwhile. He revealed to biographer Linda Hobson that he had been fond of Janet Rioch. Nevertheless, he felt that "he was somehow on the stage in that darkened room talking to her, that he was supposed to talk even when there was nothing to say."[22] There should have been much to say. The problem was Percy's reluctance to speak without a disabling fear of shame. For obvious reasons, Rioch's impression of Walker Percy cannot be ascertained. She wrote, however, one article on obstacles in transference in which the case of her brilliant, albeit disguised, southern patient almost surely emerges.[23]

No one will ever know with certainty how Walker Percy's psychoanalytic experience should be judged or indeed just how settled his opinions of psychiatry were. Depending on his artistic requirements or mood when being interviewed, he offered quite different readings. All of them made sense but showed an ambivalence toward the medical specialty that he once might have entered himself. With regard to his own treatment, the novelist recalled in conversation with Robert Coles that in 1938 he had sought advice from Harry Stack Sullivan. The psychiatrist "wasn't sure what ailed me, and I wasn't either. I must say that, after three years, five days a week, Dr. Rioch and I still weren't sure."[24] In the 1970s, Percy was particularly downhearted, partly because of the departure of his children from the nest and other factors that Jay Tolson explains in his biography. Along with religious misgivings that the biographer chronicles, Percy also turned against psychiatry. In 1974 he confessed to Barbara King, an interviewer, that he had once thought that "Freud was the answer, and he is indeed a great man." Yet, Percy added quickly, "I elevated him far beyond the point that even he would place himself." He noted that Freud himself had "said that when it comes to the ultimate mysteries of the human mind, the psychiatrist must yield to the artist, to the writer." Freud had in mind such figures as Leonardo Da Vinci and Fyodor Dostoyevsky. Unfortunately, in his opinion, the profession had become a cult, "almost a religious thing," that was entangled with "Eastern religion."[25]

In the early 1980s, however, Percy emerged from his self-dissatisfaction, and his views of psychiatric medicine turned for a time in more positive, but still skeptical, directions. On the one hand, the writer explained to interviewer Linda Hobson in 1984 that psychiatric methods of helping people to overcome mental obstacles were effective. Transference, he observed, actually works. "The analyst is able to transfer the patient's love to the outside world in a rational way." The process may even become "a kind of redemption," a high degree of "consciousness that is produced, though Freud, being a good scientist, would say 'I don't know what I'm doing except dealing with the intraphysical forces.'" Percy wrote Shelby Foote the following year that *The Interpretation of Dreams* was "a literary if not necessarily scientific masterpiece." In one of his most thoughtful articles on life in contemporary America, Percy was generous about the profession as a whole. In a show of medical snobbery, he remarked that in contrast to the amateur—"the social worker in Des Moines or the sophomore psychology student"—the expert analyst "is more apt to be eclectic," a description, perhaps, of Percy himself.[26]

Yet Percy was never wholly satisfied with the notion of manipulating the brain. Putting the words in the mouth of Tom More in *The Thanatos Syndrome,* he disputed Freud's alleged conclusion "that we are no longer sovereigns of our own consciousness."[27] He told Linda Hobson in 1981, "If I suffer anxiety and depression, my natural inclination is to go to an expert on anxiety and depression, you see." The analyst approaches the problem, Percy explained, as if it were a case of appendicitis. But the scientist is assuming an almost omnipotent role and "trying to get rid of God; he is trying to get rid of the uniqueness of man." The way scientists live, Percy complained, is to "split the world into a continuum of physical processes." Only lately, he admitted, has the study of human consciousness become a respectable subject of scientific research. In the final analysis, Percy said, the scientist cannot reach deeply into the nature of human awareness. To this he added a very curious statement. He noted how unfathomable the human sensibility is because of the mysterious character of depression, as if it were modern man's most natural state of being. "As Sartre would say," he exclaimed, "you, yourself, are the great vacuum, the great nothingness." As a Catholic, Percy constantly had to pull back from that dark conviction, but it often surfaced in his art and his public comments.[28]

Percy's physical and emotional health were intertwined. As early as his months at the Saranac sanatorium in 1942, he suffered from a sleeplessness that would plague him thereafter. His friend Shelby Foote, a lieutenant on leave from the army, had visited Percy there and found him "lonely and depressed." When tuberculosis again flared in 1955, he once more succumbed to attacks of insomnia and depression. A newly discovered drug helped him to conquer the disease. At once his spirits rose. But lack of sleep also affected him when he was otherwise well. On a trip across the continent, surrounded by friends and his wife, Bunt, Percy still found it hard to achieve that essential nightly exercise.[29] "The deeper, darker mood of despair," Tolson explains, "would erupt in strange ways." Teaching a class at Louisiana State University in 1973, for instance, Percy revealed his inner turmoil to one of his students, who recalled, "He was trying to hold everything together—his view of the world, his place in the family, his religious faith." The instructor of English 392 kept the students at a distance, although he was willing to converse about anything intellectual that struck their fancy. Then, as Wyatt Prunty, then an undergraduate, remembered, Percy astonished him one afternoon. He called to Wyatt from his office and said calmly, "Well, hello, Wyatt, I guess the central mystery of my life will be why my father killed himself. Come here, have a seat."[30] The desire to articulate the unspeakable—ordinarily in fiction—warred with the determination to keep silence and protect solitariness itself. The same contradiction seemed present in his sentiments about psychiatry, too.

Despite the conflicting perceptions of psychoanalytic medicine, Walker Percy's experience on Janet Rioch's psychiatric couch was not wasted. He showed an unusual awareness of the human dilemma. The evolution of his aŕt demonstrates the point. As D. W. Winnicott, the English analyst, once declared, psychoanalysis offers the patient "the possibility of self-knowledge" and "the opportunity for a second chance."[31] Percy's novels evolved toward ever greater maturity in the way they dealt with the interrelationship of personal and general concerns over psychiatry and medicine. At the beginning of his novelistic career, Percy did not recognize how to connect the many strands of his thought. His first effort, the unpublished novel *The Gramercy Winner,* was consciously fashioned along the lines of Thomas Mann's *The Magic Mountain.* Like Walker Percy, during his adolescence Mann had lost his stern and exacting father and suffered from nearly suicidal depressions— a family tendency that the Percys knew all too well. Yet these complications had stimulated Percy's grand literary preoccupations with the themes of conflicted sexual identity and death.[32] Nevertheless, as a novice at fiction, Percy was too preoccupied with the issue of illness and hospitalization alone and saw no larger issue than his own experience. Percy's story is set in a sylvan hospital complex that at once resembles Percy's Saranac Lake and Mann's Sanitorium Berghof. William Grey—the only northerner in Percy's stable of heroes—is a nebulous figure. Yet the novel indicated that the source of Walker's own melancholy in the early loss of his parents remained hidden from view, as if the author were still unable to deal with the family tragedy, even in fictional form. William Grey all but fails to show up for his own life. He drifts through the story as an intellectually gifted but passive spectator. The young hero's inability to mourn the death of a charismatic older friend and fellow inmate, Major Laverne Sutter, is the fundamental issue of the story. Grey whistles tunelessly as he watches his physician friends dissect Sutter's body at the coroner's office. That scene is one of the most thoroughly realized moments in an otherwise pallid novel. Percy's masterful descriptive powers were evident when he provided rich details of the cold marble slab on which the cadaver rests, the expert incisions and generous flushings of organs as they are removed, and the civilized cane-back chairs that are scattered about the room. Percy was making good use of his own experience as a resident at Bellevue Hospital. It is the only novel that he wrote in which the main character dies, but the reader learns little of Grey's inner life. Beforehand, the tubercular patient makes a new friend, a heavy-drinking, iconoclastic physician named Scanlon. In a penultimate scene, Scanlon asks Grey what makes him sad. "I don't know, Scanlon, I'm homesick." For how long, Scanlon asks. "All my life." No further revelations appear. Although there were signs of Percy's talent as a writer, he was justified in putting it aside as a failed experiment.

His first published work, *The Moviegoer,* dealt with mental rather than physical illness in a much more immediate way. Nonetheless, the sources of the depression from which both Binx Bolling and Kate Cutrer suffer are never explained in personal terms. Binx loses his father not to suicide but rather to war. Binx's father, John Bolling, has died as an airman over Crete in 1940. He leaves Binx to be reared by Aunt Emily Cutrer when the boy was fourteen, a replication of Walker's own experience in the household of the bachelor Uncle Will Percy in Greenville.[33] Yet the novel never connects the loss of a father to Binx's state of mind. Rather, he represents a generalized boredom with the routines and shallow values around him in a New Orleans suburb. Percy was not ready to overcome the taboo of familial reticence about such embarrassments as suicide, which convention designated as morally reprehensible. As a way to master his own melancholy—to give it a more externalized and perhaps less threatening character—Percy sought to objectify the issue of alienation. In his public pronouncements, he stressed the human dilemma of living in the modern age, using the sense of disengagement of a Binx Bolling as the fictional means to that end. His acceptance speech in New York for the National Book Award in 1962 that *The Moviegoer* received alluded to the issue. With regard to Binx Bolling's state of mind, Percy observed, "the pathology in this case had to do with the loss of individuality and the loss of identity at the very time when words like the 'dignity of the individual' and 'self-realization' are being heard more frequently than ever." As an intern in pathology at nearby Bellevue Hospital twenty years earlier, Percy explained to the banquet audience, his "job" had been "to stand up with a trayful of organs, lungs, liver, spleen, and such," belonging to a poor tramp. He was expected to identify their condition to his instructors. Percy drew the analogy of the hospital scene to his literary diagnosis of a world gone awry.[34] The question of existence and its meaning was for Percy very close to his own life and familial concerns, even if he refused to acknowledge that intimacy.

In the last year before he died, he still insisted to an interviewer that he had planned his first novel, *The Moviegoer*, with an abstraction in mind, not something self-revealing: "What happens to a young man with no beliefs in particular, what happens to him in the end. How he gets more in touch with life; how he goes from moviegoing to living." After the interviewer prompted him, Percy did concede, "I think we all write about ourselves more or less." He gave only a superficial account of his enforced "inactivity" at Saranac and why that might explain the plotlessness of *The Moviegoer* and its concern with depression and death. On further reflection, he admitted that tuberculosis was a serious disease even if his lesion had never been life-threatening. "You could, after all, die of it. And it was wartime too, and people were getting killed and people dying of TB, so that does make things a little more vivid." Percy's gloominess and undoubted dread of death itself at the sanatorium in the Adirondacks ran much deeper than that. Yet he refused to retreat into self-pity. His novel and his interviews about it throughout his life stressed the promise of spiritual and physical cure.[35]

His next work, *The Last Gentleman*, confronted the family history, most especially the death of Walker Percy's father. It was also more explicit than either *The Gramercy Winner* or *The Moviegoer* with regard to the reasons for the sadness and anger of the hero, Will Barrett, who followed William Grey and Binx Bolling. In *The Last Gentleman*, Barrett is young, passively distracted, and highly sensitive. He undertakes a pilgrimage of sorts to the source of his agony to recall what he had been repressing: the suicide of his father. Ed Barrett, Will remembers, had rejected his son's company although Ed had just won a victory of honor against a mob. A family celebration was in order. Finally recalling the scene toward the end of the novel, young Barrett feels the chill of a night that was supposed to be filled with happy noises as his father moves away to walk among the trees. Instead, "(Victory is the saddest of all, said the father)." However, Will realizes, "the victorious sonority of the Great Horn Theme was false, fake, fake. Underneath all was unwell."[36] What Percy implied by these words was young Will's sense of betrayal when his father turned away from him and planned his own death. The musical reference was a memory of his Uncle Will's phonograph collection of classical symphonies that Walker Percy used to play in the sad days after his father's death and mother's drowning.

The Last Gentleman also reflects Percy's concerns about physical illness, death, and medicine. A later scene in the work illustrates the point. Juxtaposed against the devastating suicide of the father is the death of Jamie Vaught, for whom Will Barrett has assumed responsibility as companion and nurse. Lying in a hospital in Santa Fe, the semiconscious boy receives the last unction from a harried Catholic priest whose bedside visit Will Barrett has arranged. After Jamie's death, Will Barrett makes explicit his selection of the half-suicidal Sutter Vaught, M.D., as the substitute father to replace the wholly suicidal one. Obviously there is an attraction to the deed even as there is also the will to live. Will Barrett even addresses Jamie's older brother in a formal way: "Dr. Vaught, I need you, I, Will Barrett," and he points to himself for emphasis. "I need you more than Jamie needed you."[37] But in fact it is Sutter who needs the most help as he contemplates his own suicide. The scene suggests Percy's major personal themes, ones that lay beneath the philosophical ones regarding redemption and the imperfections of those who seek it. In this story, even more than in the prize-winning novel *The Moviegoer,* Percy integrates the Percys' familial pattern with larger concerns in a brilliant and moving fashion.

Gratified that *The Moviegoer* and *The Last Gentleman* had established his reputation, Walker Percy had the confidence to turn to outright satire in *Love in the Ruins,* which appeared in 1971 as a Book-of-the-Month Club selection. Once again the hero, Thomas More, is a troubled figure; but for the first time in a Percy novel, the central character is himself a psychiatrist, a prospective curer of souls. A central concern in *Love in the Ruins,* very much a novel of its times, is the popular overvaluation of Dionysian license and the nationwide collapse of old certainties of faith and honor in the late 1960s. Like Sutter Vaught, Tom More seeks refuge from his own nightmares in sex. He shares his love life with three attractive women, Moira Schaffner, Lola Rhoades, and Ellen Oglethorpe. Tom More suffers from depression and fear of impotence, conditions that his lust seeks to mask. Childhood experiences are more explicitly delineated than they were in the presentation of Binx Bolling's past. Like Will Barrett and the later figure Lance Lamar in *Lancelot,* the psychoanalyst has a weak father. He is described as an alcoholic physician who had himself appointed coroner and then retired. Tom More's mother, however, is the subject of his envy. "Look at Mother!" he exclaims, "Look at the difference between us! I, a shaky decrepit forty-five, she in her sixties as pert as a sparrow and on good terms with the world." Earlier, he observes of himself, "By contrast, I am possessed by terror and desire and live a solitary life. My life is a longing, longings for women, for the Nobel Prize, for the hot bosky bite of bourbon whiskey, and other great heart-wrenching longings that have no name."[38] As Tom More explains, along with his bouts of depression, he has manic pretensions of grandeur—world recognition for inventing his magical cure-all machine, the lapsometer. Literary critic Lewis Lawson brilliantly shows how close Tom More's condition of mind is to what several psychoanalytic studies describe as the "Nobel Prize Complex," the compulsion for fame arising from Oedipal conflicts.[39] The hero was clearly and rather pathetically mad, but in tone, the novel as a whole was meant to be a romp through the extravagances of the 1960s.

Despite the temporary lift that his fame as a novelist had given him in the late sixties, there was more inner work for Walker Percy to undergo. In the following decade, gloom marked his aging as he reached his sixties. (I should add that although I stress the darker side of Percy's concerns because of the themes pursued here, he was enormously funny. His wit, of course, presents no paradox. That famous depressive Abraham Lincoln also had an appreciation of the absurdity of the human condition; melancholy has marked the great comedians in Western civilization.) In any event, Percy was acutely aware how few of his forebears had ever exceeded his own years of life. Often when he had completed a novel, a form of postpartum depression, as it were, set in. At such times, he felt very much as if life had lost meaning, and love and passion were drained. He also felt seriously distressed when he was mired down with some seemingly intractable problem in the writing process. For instance, the completion of the gothic fiction *Lancelot* proved troublesome in the mid-1970s. Percy began the work in the early 1970s, a time when (as he admitted to his daughter Ann, a student at Louisiana State University) he had been feeling low and unable to write much. "There doesn't seem to be a great deal of point," Percy told her. "Middle-age depression no doubt, plus a Percyean disposition toward melancholia." Writing *Lancelot,* which he originally called *The Knight, Death, and the Devil,* was an uphill struggle— almost "hopeless," he wrote his Catholic friend Caroline Gordon, the southern novelist.[40] Percy's own health was always a problem as well because his frame had been permanently weakened by the recurrences of tuberculosis.

While struggling with the gothic tale, he developed a case of hepatitis. It proved a blessing, however, because the ailment forced him into abstinence. For the time being, alcohol, a depressant, would not contribute to his dejection. Added to physical discomfort was his momentary alienation from the Catholic faith, which had been his anchor for so long. In the Middle Ages, monks and others seeking the divine called depression "acedia," which was thought to be the invasion of devils into the soul to introduce evil thoughts against God in the midst of their prayers. Maybe it was "male menopause or the devil," Percy wrote to Caroline Gordon. "Anyhow it takes the form in my case of disinterest, accidie [*sic*], little or no use for the things of God and the old virtues. I'd rather chase women (not that I do)."[41]

Gradually, the novel developed despite his mordancy, and he called it *Lancelot.* Its chief character, Lance Lamar, is an aristocratic plantation owner. He has murdered his wife and her lover and has tried to kill himself by blowing up his plantation mansion. Lance is obsessed with his family's past— the corruption and weakness of his father, the heritage of depression in the family, and his nostalgia for the family code. The latter upheld violence in the name of the broadsword, honorable virtues that had sustained the Lamars in America. Lance Lamar speaks in biting terms of his father's state of mind: "Secretly I believe he was afraid that of all the people on earth he alone would fail and the world would come to an end out of shame for him."[42] In making his confession to Father John Percival, Lance points out that the Lamar and Percival families were close and equally "honorable." The Lamars were convivial, hell-for-leather, and "politically active," whereas the Percivals "tended toward depression and early suicide."[43] Walker has distributed Percy characteristics to clothe the families of the two characters. Yet even in his most pessimistic novel, he closes with an affirmation. Father John, silent throughout the rambling monologue of the prisoner-patient that constitutes the text, finally utters the single word "Yes." He means that Lance Lamar, sinner though he is, can begin the road toward redemption.

In *The Second Coming,* Percy returned to the issue of hope and love in the face of mental obstacles, but personally he was far from sanguine. In 1979, confiding his thoughts to Shelby Foote, Percy observed that he had finished the draft of the work and survived it "without a catastrophe (it dying, me dying, the world coming to an end) but that's as far as I can go."[44] He continued, "I don't know whether I'm looking forward to doing a great thing like Kant and Spinoza and Verdi in the 1980s or whether I'll jump in the Bogue Falaya next week with a sugar kettle on my head (lately it's been close to the latter)." He was referring to the crazed soldier of fortune Charles Percy, who had committed suicide.[45] There was a sense of fury and frustration beneath

Percy's remark, but it also revealed the wry, deflective way that he handled those feelings. In 1987 he wrote me, "If you can't track down old Charles, Don Carlos," why not vacation on "St. Eustatia in the West Indies" and examine old records for clues about the elusive family progenitor. The first Percy wayfarer, he continued, had stopped there "on the way to Woodville, Miss. If you don't go down, I might." In signing my copy of *The Thanatos Syndrome,* he once more remarked, "I'm counting on you to find the mysterious gene."[46] The light tone did not entirely hide his interest in the subject of how depression traversed the generations.

At the same time, in nearly all his novels, Percy satirizes the hubris of those in the healing professions, most especially the psychiatrists, having almost joined their ranks himself. One is tempted to say it takes one to know one. For instance, in *The Second Coming,* he depicts the depressive heroine Allie's therapist as a doctor for the country-club set. Dr. Duk, an Anglo-Pakistani, has no clue about the sources of Allie's problem and is completely taken in by her mother, Kitty Vaught Huger. The only result of his treatment of Allie's pathological silence is to elicit a response to knock-knock jokes. With his shock treatments, he brings her nothing but pain, grief, and loneliness. Dr. Duk is as shallow in his own way as Percy's comic Episcopalian society rector, Jack Curl, is in his.[47] Rather than rely on the expertise of a smug therapist, the young Allie and the middle-aged widower Barrett find in themselves the means for their mutual rehabilitation into the life of the world. Science fails, but faith and love triumph over the evil of fallen man—and over man's propensity for melancholy—in Percy's most optimistic novel.

Having been a physician and having undergone analysis, Percy had learned how to diagnose his own condition and therefore the state of mind he wished to portray in his characters. They are Percy himself, or parts of himself. "All novels are autobiographical and all autobiographies are fiction. Writers will deny it, but it is so," novelist Harry Crews has observed. "They will claim that we shouldn't confuse the artist's life with his characters, but all the characters come out of the writer's head and reflect experiences known first-hand."[48] The fragmentation of the artist's personality that melancholia and grief seem to entail makes such imaginative antinomies possible. Analyst Arthur Rothenberg finds the essence of creativity in the ability to create "Janusian" constructions. By this term, Dr. Rothenberg means the interplay between, and even union of, opposite representations.[49] Indeed, Winnicott pointed out as early as 1951 that the universal impulse for wish-fulfilling illusion that artists transform into lasting creations "may be the essential basis for all true objectivity."[50]

In *The Thanatos Syndrome,* Percy's last novel before his death in 1990, all the themes mentioned before come together in an intense and dramatic way. Tom More, M.D., who had served prison time for prescribing drugs illegally since appearing in *Love in the Ruins,* is now wiser than before. But he is no less curious about science and its dangers and possibilities than he had been in *Love in the Ruins.* Percy depicts psychiatrist More as a former student of Janet Rioch's analyst, Harry Stack Sullivan. Yet, obviously at age forty-five, More has to be much younger than Sullivan, Uncle Will Percy's contemporary and friend. The meticulous reader might wonder how a convicted felon has regained a license to practice. Nonetheless, the chief character, as critic John Hardy observes, is "first and last" a hero named "Doctor More."[51] He is out-of-date, but proudly so. The old-fashioned shrinks have mostly lost their jobs, Tom More muses. Like Dr. Freud, he believes that "there is a psyche, that it is born to trouble as the sparks fly up." The road to recovery requires a "venturing into the heart of darkness" through hours of "talking and listening, mostly listening to another troubled human." But the old school has been superseded by "brain engineers, neuropharmacologists, chemists of the synapses." Who could complain, he asks. "If one can prescribe a chemical and overnight turn a haunted soul into a bustling little body, why take on such a quixotic quest as pursuing the secret of one's very self?"[52]

Within the framework of the novel, two themes emerge. The first and more obvious repeats Percy's social and moral concerns regarding science and modern alienation, and the second deals with equally dark aspects of the Percyean genetic past. With regard to the first, the "syndrome" to which the title refers concerns the evil work of scientists who seek to "reform" human behavior by reducing the restraints of personal guilt and promoting a policy of eugenics by which only the healthy—as the scientific bureaucrats determine that condition—are allowed to survive. They offer a sanitized version of the Nazi Holocaust. By administering doses of heavy sodium to an unsuspecting population, Bob Comeaux, one of the scientific villains, dreams of creating a utopia in which the lower orders know their place and depend on the kind of direction that planters such as Charles Percy had once seized to fashion their slaveholding world. Bob Comeaux calls his scheme a retrieval of "the best of the Southern Way of Life."[53] Just as Faulkner saw almost a divine curse on the South for its racial sins, Percy suggests a similar retribution. An old family plantation house, Belle Ame, becomes the site for hideous sexual abuses of children, as if such crimes were not only consequences of modern permissiveness but also outgrowths of the rigidly hierarchical system that produced the antebellum mansion. Tom More, aided by a very competent and rational young cousin and doctor, Lucy Lipscombe, eventually uncovers the plot and saves the world from modern science gone awry. Through Father Smith's Confession (which almost overwhelms the story), Percy shows the unchecked evolution of modern fiendishness during the era of the Second World War. The Nazis learned to hide their schemes of mass death in antiseptic, "tender" applications. Percy has Father Smith recall how in the early 1930s, Helmut, his elegant Nazi comrade, solemnly presented him with a bayonet engraved with the words "Blut und Ehre" (blood and honor).[54]

The second and more sexual confrontation with death—in the form of inherited depression—emerges from the relationship of Tom More and his medical associate, Lucy Lipscombe. She explains to her lover their odd lineage from the loins of their rascally progenitor (Charles Percy). Glad to find that Tom More is her only surviving relative aside from an old, half-crazy uncle, Lucy takes her distant cousin to "the grave of our common ancestor, an English army officer on the wrong side of the Revolution. It is a blackened granite block surmounted by an angel holding an urn." Reflecting on their forebear, Lucy says, "We come from a melancholy family. . . . He married a beautiful American girl half his age, only to have his first, English wife show up." Tom More reminds her, "He suffered spells of terrible melancholy" and persuaded himself that enemies were coming upon him in the night. The hero adds, "No wonder he jumped in the river."[55]

The Thanatos Syndrome also revealed another aspect of Percy's psychological and moral concerns. As he drew nearer to the close of his own life, he discerned in the abortion issue and in the notion of manipulated death of the elderly—in the name of tenderness and humanitarianism—a drift toward impersonal bureaucratization and mass conformity that once marched Holocaust victims to their death and would ultimately be the termination of civilized life unless an awakening of spirit emerged. His conservative position was partly a matter of Catholic faith, but it was more than that. Percy had a solicitous regard for the importance of pain in life, for meeting ordeal, dealing with tragedy without expectation of easy solutions. The pagan stoicism of his "Uncle Will" Percy had influenced him, but also important was his deep appreciation of familial agony. Like the devil tempting Christ, Bob Comeaux, a villainous scientist who seeks easy remedies for the world's ills, asks Tom More, "What would you say if I gave you a magic wand you could wave . . . and overnight you could reduce crime in the streets by eighty-five per cent?" The clever physician claims that his heavy-sodium additive to the water supply can even banish depression. By means of "pedeuthanasia" and "gereuthanasia," unwanted children and suffering old folks are to be shuffled off this mortal coil and given "a death with dignity."[56] Percy would scarcely have approved of Dr. Kevorkian.

Thus, Percy's sentiments about psychiatric medicine were mixed. On the one hand, that branch of medicine was the aspect of science that most closely resembled the subjectivity of art. Moreover, it dealt with the place of the individual in society, offering patients the chance to manage the humdrum routines—and the crises—of existence, not perfectly, but better than they had before. After all, as psychoanalyst Alan A. Stone, a president of the American Psychoanalytic Association, points out, members of his vocation are losing their faith in its scientific basis. "Those who stand on Freud's shoulders," he observes, "have not seen farther" than their giant of a master. Rather "they have seen differently." According to Stone, little of Freud's doctrines have been authenticated in experiment and study. Instead, "psychoanalysis, both as a theory and as a practice, is an art form that belongs to the humanities and not to the natural sciences. It is closer to literature than to science."[57] As Walker Percy would be quick to affirm, that conclusion scarcely means that the field is unreliable, false, or valueless. Like Freud, who used the Greek classics to describe his "scientific" findings about early human relations and workings of the mind, Percy refused to place his faith in science alone. At the same time, he was justifiably proud of his openmindedness about what science—good science as opposed to manipulative pseudoscience—could do for humankind. That flexibility and maturity of heart grew out of his own and his family's venerable intimacy with grief.

Notes

I wish to acknowledge the editorial assistance of Anne M. Wyatt-Brown, Susan Lewis, and Robert Zieger, all of whom were immensely helpful in the preparation of this essay.

1 Lewis A. Lawson, *Following Percy: Essays on Walker Percy's Work* (Troy, N.Y.: Whitsun Publishing, 1988), 228.

2 Edward Shneidman, *The Definition of Suicide: An Essay* (New York: John Wiley, 1985), 291.

3 See Lawson, *Following Percy,* 17-27; Walker Percy, *The Moviegoer* (New York: Knopf, 1961), 135.

4 Edwin Shneidman, *Suicide as Psychache: A Clinical Approach to Self-Destructive Behavior* (Northvale, N.J.: Jason Aronson, 1993), 55. See Kay Redfield Jamison, *The Unquiet Mind: A Memoir of Moods and Madness* (New York: Knopf, 1995); Mogens Schou, "Artistic Productivity and Lithium Prophylaxis in Manic-Depressive Illness," *British Journal of Psychiatry* 135 (January 1979): 97-103; Felix Post, "Verbal Creativity, De-

pression, and Alcoholism: An Investigation of One Hundred American and British Writers," *British Journal of Psychiatry* (May 1996): 545-55.

5   Stanley W. Jackson, *Melancholia and Depression, from Hippocratic Times to Modern Times* (New Haven: Yale University Press, 1986), 394; Silvano Arieti and Jules Bemporad, *Severe and Mild Depression: The Psychotherapeutic Approach* (New York: Basic Books, 1978), 224-29; *New York Times*, 20 July 1993.

6   Elliot S. Gershon, "Genetics," in Frederick K. Goodwin and Kay R. Jamison, *Manic-Depressive Illness* (New York: Oxford University Press, 1990), 373-97; George W. Arana and Steven Hyman, "Biological Contributions to Suicide," in *Suicide, Understanding and Responding: Harvard Medical School Perspectives*, ed. Douglas Jacobs and Herbert N. Brown (Madison, Conn.: International Universities Press, 1989), 73-86, esp. 77.

7   Gershon, "Genetics," 379.

8   See Anne Stevenson, *Bitter Fame: A Life of Sylvia Plath* (Boston: Houghton Mifflin, 1989); Paul Alexander, *Rough Magic: A Biography of Sylvia Plath* (New York: Viking, 1991).

9   Entry for 3 April 1932, Henry Waring Ball Diary, Mississippi Department of Archives and History, Jackson.

10   William Alexander Percy, *Lanterns on the Levee: Recollections of a Planter's Son* (1941; Baton Rouge: Louisiana State University, 1973), 57; Bertram Wyatt-Brown, *The House of Percy: Honor, Melancholy, and Imagination in a Southern Family* (New York: Oxford University Press, 1994), 25-63, 176, 175-77, 181, 194, 206, 238, 250-53, 247, 249.

11   Paul McHugh, director of the Phipps Clinic and chair of the Department of Psychiatry at the Johns Hopkins University Hospital in Baltimore, informed me that LeRoy Pratt Percy underwent the Kraepelin method of treatment, but, of course, I was not allowed to examine the thick file myself.

12   See George Zilboorg, "Differential Diagnostic Types of Suicide," *Archives of Neurological Psychiatry* 35 (1936): 270-91, and George H. Pollock, *The Mourning-Liberation Process*, vol. 1 (Madison, Conn.: International Universities Press, 1989), 155-80, 186; Wyatt-Brown, *The House of Percy*, esp. 248-55, and *The Literary Percys: Family History, Gender, and the Southern Imagination* (Athens: University of Georgia Press, 1994); Jay Tolson, *Pilgrim in the Ruins: A Life of Walker Percy* (New York: Simon and Schuster, 1992), 35-45.

13   Walker Percy, *The Message in the Bottle: How Queer Man Is, How Queer Language Is, and What One Has to Do with the Other* (New York: Farrar, Straus and Giroux, 1975), 101.

14   Tolson, *Pilgrim in the Ruins*, 96.

15   Walker Percy, interview by Bradley R. Dewey, *Conversations with Walker Percy*, ed. Lewis A. Lawson and Victor A. Kramer (Jackson: University Press of Mississippi, 1985), 5.

16   See Bertram Wyatt-Brown, "Modern Southern Writers and Russian Literature," in *Proceedings of the Fifteenth International Conference on Literature and Psychology*, ed.

Frederico Pereira (forthcoming); James L. Rice, *Dostoevsky and the Healing Art: An Essay in Literary and Medical History* (Ann Arbor, Mich.: Ardis, 1985); Daniel Rancour-Laferriere, ed., *Russian Literature and Psychoanalysis* (Philadelphia: John Benjamin, 1989).

17 Percy to Foote, January or February 1967, in *The Correspondence of Shelby Foote and Walker Percy,* 128; Percy to Foote, 22 November 1972, 168. See also Percy to Foote, 29 August 1979, 258.

18 Tolson, *Pilgrim in the Ruins,* 137–38; conversation with Alfred Kazin, Gainesville, Florida, 19 April 1987; Janet MacKenzie Rioch, "The Transference Phenomenon in Psychoanalytic Therapy," *Psychiatry* 6 (May 1943): 156.

19 Tolson, *Pilgrim in the Ruins,* 139.

20 Percy, *The Last Gentleman,* 37–38; see also Lewis A. Lawson, *Still Following Percy* (Jackson: University Press of Mississippi, 1996), 180–94.

21 Felix Brown, "Bereavement and Lack of a Parent in Childhood," in *Foundations of Child Psychiatry,* ed. Elizabeth Miller (London: Pergamon, 1968), 444, 451–54.

22 Percy, *The Last Gentleman,* 32–38; quotation, Linda Whitney Hobson, "Sign of the Apocalypse," 59.

23 Janet MacKenzie Rioch, "The Transference Phenomenon in Psychoanalytic Therapy," *Psychiatry* 6 (May 1943): 151.

24 Robert Coles, *Walker Percy: An American Search* (Boston: Little, Brown, 1979), 63.

25 Tolson, *Pilgrim in the Ruins,* 381–83; Percy, interview by Barbara King, 1974, in Lawson and Kramer, *Conversations with Walker Percy,* 94; Sigmund Freud, "Dostoevsky and Parricide," in *Sigmund Freud, Character and Culture* (New York: Macmillan, 1963), 274–93.

26 Walker Percy, "The Coming Crisis in Psychiatry," *America* 96 (5 January 1957): 391.

27 Percy, interview by Barbara King, 1974, in Lawson and Kramer, *Conversations with Walker Percy,* 94. Linda Hobson, "Study of Consciousness," 58.

28 Percy, interview by Hobson, in Lawson and Kramer, *Conversations with Walker Percy,* 224.

29 Tolson, *Pilgrim in the Ruins,* 167 (quotation), 250, 435, 455.

30 Ibid., 396.

31 Quotation in Sherry Turkle, "War Zone," review of *Winnicott,* by Adam Phillips, *London Review of Books,* 23 November 1989, 13.

32 See Nigel Hamilton, "A Case of Literary Fratricide: The Brüderzwist between Heinrich and Thomas Mann," in *Blood Brothers: Siblings as Writers,* ed. Norman Kiell (New York: International Universities Press, 1983), 49–72, esp. 60; Richard Winston, *Thomas Mann: The Making of an Artist, 1875–1911: From His Childhood to the Writing of "Death in Venice"* (New York: Simon and Schuster, 1981), 128–29; Nigel Hamilton, *The Brothers Mann: The Lives of Heinrich and Thomas Mann, 1871–1950 and 1875–1955* (New Haven: Yale University Press, 1978), 142–43.

33 Walker Percy, *The Moviegoer* (1961; New York: Farrar, Straus and Giroux, 1973), 25.

34 Walker Percy, *Signposts in a Strange Land,* ed. Patrick Samway (New York: Farrar, Straus and Giroux, 1991), 246.

35 Rebekah Presson, "Southern Semiotics: An Interview with Walker Percy (1989)," in *More Conversations with Walker Percy*, ed. Lewis A. Lawson and Victor A. Kramer (Jackson: University Press of Mississippi, 1993), 217, 218.

36 Percy, *The Last Gentleman*, 259.

37 Ibid., 409.

38 Percy, *Love in the Ruins*, 22, 168.

39 Lawson, *Still Following Percy*, 195–203.

40 Quoted in Jay Tolson, *Pilgrim in the Ruins*, 390.

41 Ibid., 393.

42 Walker Percy, *Lancelot: A Novel* (New York: Farrar, Straus and Giroux, 1977), 95–96.

43 Ibid., 5, 14–15. Lewis A. Lawson, "The Fall of the House of Lamar," in *The Art of Walker Percy: Stratagems for Being*, ed. Panthea R. Broughton (Baton Rouge: Louisiana State University Press, 1979), 219–44.

44 Walker Percy to Shelby Foote, 29 January 1979, in *The Correspondence of Shelby Foote and Walker Percy*, ed. Jay Tolson (New York: W. W. Norton, 1997), 251.

45 Walker Percy to Shelby Foote, 19 October 1973, in *The Correspondence of Shelby Foote and Walker Percy*, 180. The family legend, however, erroneously called it a sugar pot. (The Percys never raised sugar, but descendants have nicknamed Charles as "Kettle Percy.") Conversation with Eleanor Percy Gayer Merkel of Oxford, Pennsylvania, 4 August 1996.

46 Walker Percy to author, 17 July 1987, and signed copy of *The Thanatos Syndrome*, 22 June 1987, both in author's possession.

47 Percy, *The Second Coming*, 86–87.

48 Harry Crews, remarks before an undergraduate honors seminar, "Growing Up Southern: History and Literature, 1800–1965," 5 November 1987, University of Florida, Gainesville.

49 Arthur Rothenberg, *Creativity and Madness: New Findings and Old Stereotypes* (Baltimore: Johns Hopkins University Press, 1990), 15.

50 D. W. Winnicott, "Marion Milner: Critical Notice of *On Not Being Able to Paint*," in *Psychoanalytic Explorations: D. W. Winnicott*, ed. Clare Winnicott, Ray Shepherd, and Madeline Davis (Cambridge, Mass.: Harvard University Press, 1989), 391.

51 See John Edward Hardy, *The Fiction of Walker Percy* (Urbana: University of Illinois Press, 1987), 227–28, 235.

52 Walker Percy, *The Thanatos Syndrome* (New York: Farrar, Straus and Giroux, 1987), 13.

53 Ibid., 197; see also 265.

54 See William Rodney Allen, "Father Smith's Confession in *The Thanatos Syndrome*," in *Walker Percy: Novelist and Philosopher*, ed. Jan Nordby Gretlund and Karl Heinz-Westarp (Jackson: University Press of Mississippi, 1991), 195–96.

55 Percy, *The Thanatos Syndrome*, 136.

56 Ibid., 193, 197, 199.

57 Alan A. Stone, "Where Will Psychoanalysis Survive?" *Harvard Magazine*, January–February 1997, 36.

Pathology Rounds with Dr. Percy:
The Modern Malaise, Its Causes and Cure
Brock Eide

Although it were no easy matter for common people to discover for themselves the nature of their own diseases and the causes why they get worse or get better, yet it is easy for them to follow when another makes the discoveries and explains the events to them. . . . It is my intention to discuss what man is and how he exists because it seems indispensable for a doctor to have made such studies and to be fully acquainted with Nature.—Hippocrates, *Tradition in Medicine*

Little things can be important. Even more important is the ability—call it a knack, hunch, providence, good luck, whatever—to know what you are looking for and to put two and two together.—Walker Percy, *The Thanatos Syndrome*

It is in some ways ironic that anyone should collect a book of essays on the topic of "Walker Percy, Physician." Percy, as others have pointed out, never actually practiced medicine, except for two years of medical school clerkships and a few short months of pathology internship; and by his own admission, he didn't much like the few brief exposures he had. In fact, in later life he often referred to the tuberculosis that ended his medical career with a kind of fond gratitude, implying that it had saved him from a fate worse than, well, pulmonary tuberculosis.

Given his distaste for medical practice, it might seem unlikely that even academic fancy could squeeze much mileage from "Percy as Physician." Yet to those familiar with both Percy's writings and the practice of medicine (such as the contributors to this volume), such a topic seems neither pointless nor farcical. In fact, there are good reasons to think that a book about "Walker Percy, Physician," could be a valuable addition to Percy scholarship, even when comparable works on the youthful occupations of other authors—such as "T. S. Eliot, Banker," "Franz Kafka, Insurance Clerk," or "Charles Dickens, Court Stenographer"—would not. This is, no doubt, because there is something in Percy's writings very much reminiscent of what it is that doctors do. I believe this "something" is related to medicine's nature as a learned profession with its own characteristic method of investigation and practice. Like medicine, Percy's writings are concerned with discovering the mechanisms and the standards of healthy human functioning, with diagnosing and characterizing forms of pathological dysfunction, and with restoring the dysfunctional to normal health; but whereas medicine is concerned with human health in a very broad sense, Percy was concerned primarily with the health of the human self.

Percy's fascination with the human self is in many ways at the heart of all his writings—both fiction and nonfiction—and only those who have firmly grasped his views on the nature and health of the human psyche can properly understand his works. In this essay, I would like to consider Percy's views on these topics as expressed in his works, beginning where he often did, with an examination of the particular form of psychopathology he believed most characteristic of our time.

One of the things Percy found most surprising about human beings—and especially modern ones—is how many of us seem to feel out of place and anxious in what appears to be our natural environment. This seemed to him especially remarkable given that modern scientific accounts of human nature—which Percy saw as providing the dominant mythos of our age—tell us that we, like our fellow creatures, are simply organisms in an environment with a certain number of needs that require satisfaction for organismal homeostasis. Anxiety on such accounts is simply a manifestation of unmet biological needs, and the meeting of these needs on this account produces the sense of well-being. But Percy, both on the basis of his own observation and personal experiences, came to doubt these accounts. In his experience, it was not only possible but even common for human beings to experience anxiety, boredom, restlessness, aimlessness—even a vague desire to somehow "transcend the merely human"—even though their basic needs for food, sex, and rest, and even their higher "needs" for friendship, play, creative activity, beneficence, and knowledge, had been satisfied. In fact, Percy came to believe that such feelings are typical of contemporary human experience, a characteristic "modern malaise," the resolution of which is in many ways the central problem of our existence.

Percy was critical of the tendency of modern science to treat these feelings as essentially meaningless epiphenomena—as complex disorders of brain chemistry or artifacts of evolution, adaptive in some former age but now mere vestigial hangovers, emotional equivalents of the appendix. He saw such feelings as possessing tremendous epistemic value, as pointing us to our true nature and fulfillment. Consequently he believed that the tendency to deny their significance greatly contributed to the widespread psychic unrest apparent in contemporary society. For Percy, such feelings are symptoms of a profound psychic conflict, and this conflict can be resolved only if we heed what our anxieties are telling us about ourselves. Failure to listen will inevitably worsen the conflict, and we will lose any chance for psychic growth, harmony, integration, and fulfillment. Only two alternatives will remain: first, we can ignore these feelings as meaningless, probably on the advice of a so-called expert; or second, we can drown them out by diversions, whether sensual, aesthetic, intellectual, or even spiritual. According to Percy, both these alternatives must inevitably fail to heal our primary disorder.

Percy's best portrait of a person using such defenses is no doubt Binx Bolling, the protagonist of *The Moviegoer*. Whether leafing through tomes by famous materialist scientists, or taking inspiration from humanitarian credos recited on the radio show "This . . . I Believe," or going to movies in faceless suburbs, or sporting around with an endless succession of secretaries in his little red MG, Binx displays a nearly Edisonian inventiveness in finding ways to "defeat" the malaise. But Percy saw such alternatives as at best merely enabling us to repress our anxieties and get along in the world like most everyone else: holding jobs and raising families, consuming life's goods and services, coping with life's unpleasantness, persisting more or less intact, being more or less "functional." But at worst such alternatives fail, either because they are simply overwhelmed by some sudden catastrophe—such as Binx Bolling's wounding on the battlefield in Korea, or Kate Cutrer's vision of her fiancé's mangled corpse—or because they have gradually been worn away by a slow, unremitting assault, like *The Last Gentleman*'s Will Barrett's slide into psychosis during his college years. Either way, when such defenses fail, we are left to confront our anxieties head-on.

In this defenseless posture, we have few options. Some are better than others, but from Percy's perspective, only one of them is any good. Each is exemplified in his fiction. Suicide is the first option, and the one chosen by Will Barrett's father in *The Last Gentleman* when he realized tragically that his traditional cavalier virtues could never win out against the small-mindedness and petty vice of the New South. Collapse into debilitating psychopathology is the second, as seen in Will himself in both *The Last Gentleman* and *The Second Coming* when he was haunted by a memory he could not face, by Lance Lamar in *Lancelot* when he was confronted by his wife's infidelity, and by Allie, Will's young love, in *The Second Coming*. Scabrous nihilism is the third, as portrayed most vividly in *The Last Gentleman*'s Sutter Vaught, whose clear vision of human depravity in the absence of hope has plunged him into anger and cynicism. Stoic resignation or tragic posturing is the fourth, as shown unforgettably in Binx's Aunt Emily in *The Moviegoer,* who is determined defiantly to impose her will on an otherwise orderless world. The fifth option, and the only good one, is one that we usually pursue only when these other defensive postures have failed: We can believe—at least provisionally—that our anxieties might be telling us something about who we are, about why we came to be troubled in the first place, and about what we might do to put ourselves right again. We may, as Percy said, begin a search—a search for clues regarding the meaning of our disordered state.

For those who decide to embark on such a search, one question immediately arises: What should one look for? In a way, the answer seems only too obvious: something that will resolve the predicament that prompted the search in the first place. But such an answer is practically worthless because it fails to tell us what that "something" might be, or how and where we should look for it. It's like going to your doctor and saying, "Doctor, I don't feel well," and hearing the reply, "Then you'd better do something about your health." Not exactly wrong, but not why you sat there for two hours reading back issues of *Field and Stream,* either. What you want—what you *need*—is an accurate diagnosis of your disorder and a proper plan of therapy. To arrive at these things, your doctor must first employ a knowledge of normal human health to see where your condition deviates from the norms: "Wrenching pain in your gut? That's not normal in a healthy person. Probably the sign of a pathological disorder. Let's ask a few more questions and run a few tests, and we'll learn what's wrong with you and what to do about it."

For Percy also, we can discover the cause (or causes) of the modern malaise and (we hope) find its cure only once we have discovered what constitutes the health of the human self. Percy felt that the best way to arrive at such knowledge was by simply looking at human beings to see what kinds of creatures they are—what they do, what they desire, what they need, what seems to be good for them (and bad); in other words, to discover something about human nature. For Percy, this was best done by starting with the facts most clearly at hand: that is, with the experiences each one of us has in living as a unique and uniquely human self. Percy proposed that we examine such experiences, looking for recurring patterns and underlying themes. From these, we could distill an understanding of human nature that would harmonize and explain our observations. In short, Percy proposed that we create a "phenomenology of the self," or what he termed an "anthropology in the European sense."

Percy began his examination of human nature with the aspect of human functioning that he believed both most remarkable and most important for self-understanding: the use of symbolic language.[1] Beginning in the mid-1950s and continuing until his death in 1990, Percy developed his views on the nature and significance of human language both in his novels and in an extensive array of nonfiction works. In many ways, Percy's thoughts on language form a sort of intellectual Amazonian rain forest: lush, exotic, rich in wonders and hidden curatives, but also dense, overgrown, tangled—a place where progress is measured in inches and the faint of heart quickly bog down.[2] No short treatment could possibly do justice to the depth and extent of this thought, and it is a significant challenge to make even small portions of it clear in a limited space. Given this complexity, I will limit my focus to the one aspect of human symbolic language that Percy saw as revealing most about human nature itself: that is, its apparent irreducibility to the kind of two-component cause-and-effect relationship characteristic of every other known phenomenon in the universe.

For Percy, human speech is absolutely unique in kind, having no parallel in nature, and as such it is particularly important for anyone wanting to understand human nature. Following the American philosopher Charles Sanders Peirce, Percy saw human language as embodying a three-component, or "triadic," relationship, the three components being the symbol-using human, the object to be symbolized, and the symbol[3] employed by the human to represent the object. Already I see the vines creeping around us, and our feet sinking into the mud, so let me see if I can make this a little clearer with two illustrations from Percy.

First, take the case of a boy and a small red ball. When the boy asserts that this small red object "is a ball," he stands in relation both to the physical ball and to the word "ball" as a separate and distinct entity, just as the ball itself is distinct from the word "ball." There are three distinct entities: the boy, the ball, and the word (or symbol) "ball."

Second, consider the famous story about the moment when Helen Keller first understood what language is. There she stood by an outdoor pump, feeling on one hand the rushing of water, feeling on the other Anne Sullivan impressing the characters "W-A-T-E-R," and suddenly realizing with a flash of insight that the one was meant to be or to symbolize the other. For Peirce and Percy, there were three distinct entities involved in that interaction: the physical water, the word or symbol "water," and Helen, as it were, in the middle, coupling the two together.

According to Percy, this triadic relationship is characteristic of most human speech, and it is fundamentally irreducible to the kind of two-component, or "dyadic," relationship that characterizes all other natural phenomena, including animal language. Perhaps this can be seen more clearly if we consider for a moment Percy's depiction of a young child's progression from dyadic to triadic speech:

> A father tells his two-year old child [who is still using exclusively a dyadic mode of speech] that *this,* pointing to a certain object, is a ball. The child understands him, and whenever his father speaks the word, the child looks for the ball and runs to get it. But this is not [triadic speech]. The child's understanding is not qualitatively different from the understanding which a dog has of the word "ball"; it can be construed in terms of response conditioning, sound waves, neural impulses, brain patterns. It is, in other words, a sequence of happenings which takes place among material beings and is, in this respect, not utterly different from a solar eclipse, glandular secretion, or nuclear fusion.
>
> But one day the father utters the word "ball" and his son suddenly understands that his father does not mean find the ball, or where is the ball, but, rather, this *is* a ball—the word "ball" *means* this round thing.
>
> Something has happened.[4]

For Percy, the child has made the transition from dyadic speech, which can be explained like any other event in the universe as the consequence of a chain of two-component interactions, like a series of billiard balls sequentially colliding and setting each other in motion, to triadic speech, which cannot by any manipulation or invention be so understood. The word "ball" has been given a life of its own, separable from a particular object, and it can be used in an essentially infinite variety of new ways: to think abstractly about "balls," to define their characteristics, to poetically conjure up images of other round things, and so forth.

Percy's belief that human language embodied a unique triadic relationship put him profoundly at odds with most other midcentury American linguistic theorists, whose theories were based on dyadic, or two-component simple cause-and-effect, mechanisms.[5] Such theories tried to explain human language—whether at the neuronal or higher psychological levels—as arising from the same kind of "A-to-B" energy-exchange reactions that modern science posited as the basis for all other known phenomena; even psychoanalytic theories of human symbolizing invoke a struggle between subconscious forces that can be visualized in simple cause-and-effect fashion. But according to Percy, human language can simply not be understood in this fashion.

The problem—or, for Percy, the wonder—is that there is in addition to the object and its word-symbol this third *thing,* this "coupler." According to Percy, no matter how hard one tries, this coupler cannot simply be gotten rid of, even though dyadic theories inevitably ignore it. For Percy, however, this coupler is crucially important. He saw it as in some way intimately connected with, and perhaps even the locus of, the human self. For Percy, this coupler is the source of the sense that we have when speaking that we are free to say "A" rather than "B," or that we can assent or dissent to a given proposition. This freedom is simply not explainable by two-component, cause-and-effect-based theories because they must inevitably make "my answer" to "your question" a kind of reflex response rather than an act of choice or free will. Percy realized that this "coupler-self" could not be demonstrated "scientifically" as a material entity, but he nonetheless believed that it could be proven to exist by a consideration of the logical requirements of language itself (as just outlined).

This finding of a coupler-self buried beneath the everyday phenomenon of human speech is the key to Percy's fascination with linguistics—a fascination his readers have often had difficulty sharing. But for Percy, the nature of human speech and the existence of this coupler-self have profound implications for our understanding of human nature and experience. Indeed, Percy believed that a thorough consideration of triadic speech and of the kind of human nature it required would tell us volumes about the kind of creatures we are and where the source of our feelings of alienation lies. Such a consideration is difficult and more than a little complex, but as it is central to Percy's thought, we must do our best to follow.

For Percy, it is solely through triadic or symbolic speech that we are able to think abstractly and to acquire our conceptual knowledge. Such knowledge is important because it enables us to live not simply as organisms in an environment, conscious only of those things possessing immediate biological significance, but as selves in a world, which we understand by representing it to ourselves through symbols. (This symbolic "world" should be understood as comprehending all of reality, not just physical nature, as in the ancient Greek *cosmos.*) According to Percy, insofar as our understanding of the world is accurate, our beliefs will be consistent with our experience, and we will be able to make sense both of the world and of our place in it. This will result in a kind of psychic harmony, in the sense that we will be free from feelings of alienation and the anxieties they produce. This does not necessarily mean that we will be happy in any conventional sense, for we may learn things that are quite unpleasant. Nevertheless we will still be better off, for a true knowledge of ourselves and of the world is the only true road to human fulfillment: Like Will Barrett in *The Second Coming*, we must understand and become reconciled to the deepest truths about ourselves and our world—no matter how unpleasant—if we are ever to learn how we must order our lives. Our only alternative is to adopt a false "understanding" of the world and of ourselves, and if we choose this option, our beliefs will be discordant with our experiences, and we will be made to feel like aliens in our own world.

Unfortunately, everyone is at least initially in this position of alienation, for according to Percy, there is one thing in our world that we can never accurately symbolize: our own selves.[6] According to Percy, no one can adequately symbolize his or her own self because that self is simply too "mobile" or "freed up"—too able to assume an infinite range of apparent identities or symbolic forms.[7] Percy gave the following humorous example of how our self-conception can simultaneously cover all poles of the compass—which is to say, no place at all—in *Lost in the Cosmos*:

> You are an Aries. You open your newspaper to the astrology column and read an analysis of the Aries personality. It says, among other things:
> "You have the knack of creating an atmosphere of thought and movement, unhampered by petty jealousies. But you have the tendency to scatter your talents to the four winds."
> Hm, you say, quite true. I'm like that.
> Suddenly you realize you've made a mistake. You've read the Gemini column. So you go back to Aries:
> "Nothing hurts you more than to be unjustly mistreated or suspected. But you have a way about you, a gift for seeing things through despite all obstacles and distractions. You also have a desperate need to be liked. So you have been wounded more often than you will admit."
> Hm, you say, quite true. I'm like that.
> The . . . question is: Why is it that both descriptions seem to fit you— or, for that matter, why do you seem to recognize yourself in the self-analysis of all twelve astrological signs?[8]

For Percy, this inability firmly to locate the self under any one set of descriptors is the common lot of human beings, and he referred to this problem as the "unique unformulability of the self." This "unique unformulability" has at least two important consequences: first, as soon as a self discovers its own unique unformulability within the world of symbols, the self becomes acutely conscious of its own existence (or self-conscious); second, it becomes aware of its essential difference from the rest of the world (or alienated). For Percy, it was the self's awareness of its own essential difference from the rest of the world that produces the feelings of malaise, anxiety, boredom, restlessness, discontent, and homelessness with which he was so concerned.

Such feelings, Percy believed, affect us all at one time or another, so we must all try to deal with them as best we can. Percy saw most modern attempts as falling into one of two very general categories, both of which were inevitably doomed to failure because they are based on inadequate understandings of the self.

Percy called the first of these the strategy of "immanence." To understand this strategy, we must first remember that for Percy, the human sense of alienation arises from the self's inability *truly* to symbolize itself. In this strategy, the self tries to compensate for this inability by adopting a *false* identity, claiming to be something that *is* easily symbolized in hopes that it can now "place" itself (or become immanent) in its world of symbols. The identity most often claimed by modern selves, according to Percy, is that of an organism in an environment—a kind of consumer-self whose goal in life is simply to achieve the satisfaction of its various biological and interpersonal needs. In adopting this identity, the individual essentially attempts to deny that there is anything problematic about his or her place in the world: "The experts say I'm just a self with certain needs? Then that's what I am. If I feel any anxiety, I'll take it as a sign of unmet biological or interpersonal needs and consume some more." Such a strategy may enable us to repress our symptoms of alienation, even for an extended period of time; but according to Percy, such a victory is Pyrrhic, for even if we do succeed in repressing our feelings of alienation (and quite often we do not), the most we can hope for is an impoverished and limited sort of life, one that for Percy is ultimately less than fully human. For Percy, such a self saves itself only by pretending to be less than it truly is, and in his eyes, this is the worst fate possible for a human being. It is a despair so hopeless it does not even realize it is despair, and the tragedy of this despair is that it cuts us off entirely from any possibility of attaining our true purpose as human beings.

The second common strategy for avoiding the problem of alienation is the peculiarly modern search for "transcendence." In this strategy, the self tries to relieve its sense of homelessness in the world by attempting to escape the world altogether. As in the strategy of immanence, the individual assumes a false identity: the self as pure knower, disconnected, separated from the world. In the modern world, transcendence is sought most commonly through activity in the arts and sciences.

The scientist, according to Percy, achieves transcendence by abstracting his or her own self from the world and looking down on the world, as it were, from outside—by "going into orbit" around it, in Percy's terminology. The scientist's own self is thus banished from nature and temporarily forgotten in the absorption of discovery, and the rest of the world is made to appear a completely explicable closed dyadic system. As long as the scientist can maintain this transcendent orbit—that is, as long as he or she is able to remain absorbed in the objective posture of the creative scientist—the problem of alienation is essentially put on hold.

The artist, in contrast, attempts to achieve transcendence by precisely the opposite path: by directly confronting and contemplating the problem of the self. The artist's vocation is to give voice to the previously unspeakable predicament of the self in the modern world—that is, to document "the strange and feckless movements of the self trying to escape itself."[9] While engaged in creative activity, the artist is temporarily able to become lost in his or her own objectification of the self, and in so doing to forget the despair of alienation.

For Percy, however, the strategy of transcendence is inherently problematic because the transcendent posture is difficult to maintain—for both artists and scientists—and when there is a pause in their creative work, as there nearly always must be, their transcendent "orbits" tend to "decay." Such decay occurs when the self is no longer able to convince itself that it is entirely separate from the world it inhabits—that is, when it must "traffic with immanence": deal with other selves, earn a living, care for the body, gratify the appetites. In such situations, the self is forced to "reenter" the world of immanence, and it must try (as we saw earlier) to locate itself within the world of symbols. Such reentries are not easy, as Percy explains in *Love in the Ruins,* for when "a person has so abstracted himself from himself and from the world around him, seeing things as theories and himself as a shadow . . . he cannot, so to speak, reenter the lovely ordinary world. Instead he orbits the earth and himself. Such a person, and there are millions, is destined to haunt the human condition like the Flying Dutchman."[10] The best the transcending self can do is to adopt the posture of an immanent organism in an environment (as we saw in our consideration of immanence). But in many ways, this posture is far more difficult to strike for a self that has known transcendence than for one that has not, and such selves face severe difficulties. For Percy, one of the means that contemporary transcending selves use most commonly to "reenter the sphere of immanence" is sexual activity: the "sole concrete metaphysic of the layman in the age of science = the sacrament of the dispossessed."[11] Percy vividly portrays the difficulties faced by an individual who must oscillate between the orbit of transcendence (as attained through the arts and sciences) and the sphere of immanence (as reentered through "genital sexuality") in *The Last Gentleman*'s Dr. Sutter Vaught. Vaught ruminates at length in a private journal on the problems posed by immanence and transcendence. In one rambling, boozy entry, he explains why sex is his only available avenue for "reentry from the orbit of transcendence": "Science, which (in layman's view) dissolves concrete things and relations, leaves intact touch of skin to skin. Relation of genital sexuality reinforced twice: once because it is touch, therefore physical, therefore 'real'; again because it corresponds with theoretical (i.e., sexual) substrata of all other relations. Therefore genital sexuality = twice 'real.'" [12]

In other words, by reducing the (triadic) meaning of human relationships to the (dyadic) level of biological reactions and subconscious psychological forces, science (or at least the popular forms of pseudoscience) has reduced that which is "real" both in human interactions and in human beings themselves to pure physicality. To the extent that one can accept such a view of the human, one will be able to reenter the sphere of immanence. But for those who have known the possibility of transcendence, this is very unlikely. Indeed, they will be far more likely to enhance their own awareness of the gap that exists between their transcendent knowing self and their immanent bodily self, worsening their symptoms of alienation.

Besides these two strategies, we can also, according to Percy, try to deal with the problem of our self's unformulability and our consequent alienation by turning to religion. Certain religions appear promising because they offer the self an identity that is easily placed within the world of signs. Two examples that Percy cited are totemism, in which the self is identified with some readily symbolizable object or ideal description (such as an Aleut Indian's identification of himself as "a bear" or an actress's identification of herself as "a Libra"), and Eastern pantheism, in which the self is identified with God and nature. But for Percy, such religions ultimately prove inadequate because, like the strategies of immanence and transcendence, they create for the self a false, rather than true, identity.

For Percy, there is only one way fully to resolve the problem of our identity and to deal with our symptoms of alienation, and that is belief in one of the "theistic-historical" religions of Christianity, Judaism, and Islam. Through such religions, Percy believed, "the self becomes itself by recognizing God as . . . creator of the Cosmos, and therefore one's self as a creature . . . who shares with a community of like creatures a belief in that God, who transcends the entire Cosmos and has actually entered human history—or will enter it—in order to redeem man from the catastrophe which has overtaken his self."[13] According to Percy, this catastrophe consists, at least in part, in our loss of the knowledge that we were created by God for fellowship with Him and our inability to recover that knowledge without divine grace and revelation. We are, in other words, in the position of a castaway washed up on a strange island with no memory of who we are or where we came from.

Percy employed the image of the castaway frequently in his writings, but he developed it most thoroughly in his essay "The Message in the Bottle" in the book of the same name. He begins with a castaway who comes to himself on an island that he finds to be inhabited by a more or less friendly and advanced civilization. Gradually he is taken into their community, participating in their industries, cultural institutions, and social relationships, but he can never shake the sense that this is not his true home—that he is in fact a castaway. He explores his new surroundings, hoping to find some clue as to his own identity. In the course of his investigations, he discovers something interesting: Each night, a number of bottles wash up on the beach, each containing a single sentence written on a slip of paper. He develops the habit of going each morning to the beach to collect these bottles, for there is something about the messages that intrigues him. As he accumulates these messages, he finds that some excite his interest more than others, and he wonders why. The interesting messages do not differ from the others on simply logical grounds, such as the analytic/synthetic distinction. They also do not differ along typical "scientific" grounds, such as being "testable" or not. Instead, they seem to separate out according to their relevance to his particular situation—which is to say, to his predicament as a castaway. Furthermore, he finds that the statements that seem most relevant to his situation share a particular quality: they express a state of affairs that is by its nature contingent. These can be a claim about either some historical fact, or the intentions of some agent, or the existence or nature of some person, place, or thing, all of which may be true but are neither logically necessary nor scientifically demonstrable by the castaway in his current position. The castaway is uncertain at first what to call such statements but finally settles on the name "news," for such statements are bits of data that cannot be obtained by any effort of indirect experimentation, reflection, or artistic endeavor, but only by direct observation or the report of witnesses. Take, for example, one of the statements that the castaway categorizes as news: "There is potable water in the next cove." How could he know this to be true? Not by consulting the periodic table or calculating the density of water; not by reasoning down from first principles regarding the nature of islands and thirst; not by reflecting on the human desire for water and the gracious care of Nature for her children; but only by being told that there was water by someone who had seen it, or by going to look himself.

Now, whether the castaway receives a *particular* message as news depends first on his perception that he is in a predicament and second on his openness to the very possibility of receiving news. A perfectly contented castaway will never receive any message as a piece of news, for no message could possibly be relevant to his situation. Similarly, a purely objective-minded castaway who is concerned only with the truth or falsity of the messages but never with their relevance to his situation would never see any message as news. Only the castaway who *sees* his need and dares to hope that some message might possibly relieve his predicament will be open to the possibility of news.

To the extent that the castaway *does* perceive some message as a piece of news (i.e., as relevant to relieving his predicament), it will provide him with a reason for action. But it is important to note that any message he decides to act on *must* be acted on *before* his ability to verify its truth, for there is simply no other means of verification available, and his need is desperate (he is in a predicament). He will act, even in the absence of perfect knowledge, because he quite simply has no other choice. Verification (or refutation) of the message will be had, to be sure, but not before the castaway has taken the risk of acting on it.

Percy gives us a portrait of such a stranded self in the figure of Will Barrett in *The Last Gentleman.* Alienated from himself and from his world, far from home and living alone in a Manhattan YMCA, passing his days aimlessly, not knowing who he is or what he should do with his life, the young Will is a castaway desperate for news. Percy describes the young man and his situation as follows:

> It did not take him long to act. Often nowadays people do not know what to do and so live out their lives as if they were waiting for some sign or other. This young man was such a person. If a total stranger had stopped him this morning on Columbus Circle and thrust into his palm a note which read: *Meet me on the NE corner of Lindell Blvd and Kings Highway in St. Louis 9 A.M. next Thursday—have news of utmost importance,* he'd have struck out for St. Louis (the question is, how many people nowadays would not?) [14]

But just because the castaway is desperate, he will not, according to Percy, act on every piece of news simply because it purports to be relevant to his situation. Instead, he will act only on those that seem to bear the proper "credentials" of truth. Such messages must possess two fundamental characteristics: they must appear to be at least possibly true, and they must be presented by the bearer with a sobriety and reasonableness that suggests that the bearer is likely to be trustworthy. If both characteristics are present, the castaway will act, for his need for help is desperate.

According to Percy, we are all in the position of the castaway, strangers in a world not our home. And because it is not truly our home, we may find, even after we have done everything possible to make ourselves feel at home— whether by satisfying our bodily and emotional needs, or losing ourselves in intellectual endeavor, or "finding ourselves" through popular religion or psychology—that we are left with the unshakable feeling that "something is wrong . . . something is missing." We may find, in other words, that we are like the castaway, who "in his heart of hearts can never forget who he is: a stranger, a castaway, who despite a lifetime of striving to be at home on the island is as homeless now as he was the first day he found himself cast up on the beach." If we find ourselves in such a predicament, the worst thing we can do, according to Percy, is pretend that our alienation is fundamentally meaningless, and that we really are at home in this world; for as Percy learned from Kierkegaard, "the worst of all despairs is to imagine one is at home when one is really homeless." We can find our true place in the world only if we discover the true nature of our alienation.

For Percy, this discovery can come only in the form of news from our "true home," which is, as he wrote in *The Message in the Bottle,* "across the sea." Only news from this source can tell us what we most deeply need and want to know: who we are as human selves, and what we must do to live as we should. According to Percy, such news is presented in its fullest form only in the Christian Gospels: the "Good News" of salvation, delivered by the witness of the apostolic news bearers, who were actual firsthand witnesses to the truth of the message. Only such news can enable the self to know itself as it truly is—that is, as God knows it, and as He created it to be. Percy believed that the self could find its true identity only through reconciliation with God, and he often approvingly quoted these words of Kierkegaard: "The self can only become itself if it does so transparently before God." [15]

This is the final linking of spiritual and phenomenal categories that was at the heart of Percy's intentions as an author: the self, which was lost to itself through its inability to understand itself, is recovered by finding its true nature in God. Percy knew this assertion was not scientifically testable or logically self-justifying. He saw it instead as knowledge acquired by experience whose justification his readers would have to provide by their own experiences. For Percy, such experiential knowledge was given very high respect. In fact, in areas involving human meaning and purpose—the

"whys" of our existence rather than the "whats," "whens," and "hows"—
it was the highest form of knowledge possible. This points to an important
aspect of Percy's Christian beliefs: He did not believe because he thought
Christianity's tenets could be logically or scientifically verified; he believed
because the central mysteries of his own existence were rendered clearer
through the lens of Christian teaching. It was for Percy as it was for Augus-
tine in his famous *credo ut intelligam:* "I believed that I might understand;
and when I understood, I believed." This is not, as it has often been misinter-
preted by Freud and others, an admission of the irrationality of faith. Rather,
it is an honest recognition that we as human beings do not have transparent
access to the first principles of knowledge, and that consequently, before we
can know anything about the world, we must first make certain assumptions
from which we can begin to reason. We must, in other words, choose for ourselves a standpoint from which we will view the world—we cannot simply,
as philosopher Thomas Nagel has pointed out, choose to view the world
from nowhere. And the way we determine that we have picked the best view-
point is by finding—only once we are there—that from our new position,
we can see the world more clearly and make better sense of it than we can
from any other spot. For Percy, Christianity was true because its answers to
the questions that most haunted him—who he was and how he should live
in this world—made greatest sense in light of his own experiences. Christianity for Percy was fundamentally a form of knowledge, pointed to and
verified by human experience, not a blind and desperate leap of faith, and
he utterly separated his own beliefs from Kierkegaard on this point. Christianity for Percy was true because it brought together the disparate strands
of his deepest self—strands that were ignored or discarded in other explana-
tory systems—and wove them into a single, unified fabric, giving his life a
sense of wholeness and completeness it had previously lacked. And this uni-
fying, clarifying power of the Christian message is reflected, however subtly,
in nearly everything he wrote.

My purpose in this essay is not to claim that Percy's novels are merely
religious allegories, or that his nonfiction works are thinly veiled tracts. On
the contrary, the religious themes in his novels are so unobtrusive that they
are missed by the majority of his readers,[16] and his linguistic studies have
attracted scholarly interest quite unrelated to their religious implications.
Rather, my intent is simply to acknowledge that the animating desire for his
literary career and the deepest themes of his life's work must ultimately be
understood in light of his religious faith.

Neither should such statements be taken to imply that Percy's writings
will hold interest only for those sympathetic with his religious beliefs. In

fact, Percy's depictions of human alienation and anxiety and his naming of the human predicament have given pleasure, relief, and the comfort of fellowship to numerous readers who lack his faith, and Percy was genuinely pleased that his writings were able to do so. But in the final analysis, Percy's highest aim was to share the message that he believed had saved his life. As the former physician wrote early in his career to his writing mentor Caroline Gordon: "What I really want to do is to tell people what they must do and what they must believe if they want to live." This desire was to animate Percy's writing for the rest of his career.

Notes

1 For Percy' reasoning along these lines, see especially the essays "The Delta Factor," in *The Message in the Bottle* (New York: Noonday, 1992), and "Is a Theory of Man Possible?" in *Signposts in a Strange Land*, ed. Patrick Samway (New York: Farrar, Straus and Giroux, 1991). See also Percy's "Semiotic Primer of the Self," in *Lost in the Cosmos* (New York: Noonday, 1983), 85.

2 Percy, being Percy, would no doubt want to know where I thought the poison tree frogs were hidden.

3 Percy sometimes used the term "symbol" as I have here; at other times, he employed the term "sign" or even "signal" and used "symbol" for another purpose. These distinctions are (fortunately) not important for this introduction to Percy's thought, and I will use only the word "symbol."

4 Percy, "Naming and Being," in *Signposts in a Strange Land,* 130.

5 Although Percy believed that human speech was absolutely unlike any other form of communication known in embodying triadic behavior, he did not hold (at least in his later years) that the importance of human speech lay in its uniqueness per se. See, e.g., *Lost in the Cosmos,* 95: "The present argument does not require that triadic behavior be unique in man. Perhaps it is not. [This theory] proposes only that where triadic behavior occurs, certain new properties and relationships come into existence."

6 At least without assistance. (See hereafter.)

7 *Lost in the Cosmos,* 107.

8 Ibid., 5.

9 Ibid., 120.

10 Percy, *Love in the Ruins* (New York: Ivy, 1971), 29.

11 Percy, *The Last Gentleman* (New York: Noonday, 1966), 279.

12 Ibid., 280.

13 *Lost in the Cosmos,* 112.

14 *The Last Gentleman,* 6.

15 As quoted in *Lost in the Cosmos,* 156.

16 A fact that Percy occasionally lamented.

Walker Percy, Reluctant Physician

Jay Tolson

My visit with Walker Percy in the late autumn of 1989 had the melancholy feel of a last farewell. By then we both knew that he was dying of the cancer that had started in his prostate and quickly spread to other parts of his body. He talked matter-of-factly about his approaching end—not with any false heroism but with a doctor's clarity about the mechanism of the disease running its all but inevitable course. Again and again during those days, I was reminded of Maxim Gorky's poignant words about his fellow artist and countryman Anton Chekhov, who faced death with a similar clear-sightedness: "He was a doctor—and illness for a doctor is always harder to bear than for a patient: the patient only feels, while the doctor, in addition to feeling, knows the processes by which the organism is destroyed. In such cases we may consider knowledge as causing the approach of death."

I'm not sure that Percy's knowledge hastened the course of his disease, but I think it made him a little more ruthless in the way he went about detaching himself from the world, particularly from those things that implied a future from which he knew he would be excluded. His wife Bunt had recently bought him a portable computer, which, at the time of my visit, sat amid a disarray of boxes, packing materials, and instructions on the dining table in their large living and dining area. She had hoped that he might use the computer on future trips to the Mayo Clinic, where he had been going for chemical therapy—"a new drug combo," as Percy described it to Shelby Foote in a letter dating from the previous July, "(something called interferon and 5-FW) said to be promising in some cancers." But in that same letter to his oldest friend, Percy had confessed to his growing distaste for the medical ordeal:

> The worst thing is the travelling and hospitals. Flying around the U.S. is awful and hospitals are no place for anyone, let alone a sick man. . . . What is a pain is not even the pain but the nuisance. It is a tremendous bother (and expense) to everyone. Worst of all is the indignity. Who wants to go to pot before strangers, be an object of head shaking for

friends, a lot of trouble to kin? I know the answer to this of course: false pride—who are you to be too proud to go the way of all flesh—or as you would write at Bellevue:—"the patient went rapidly downhill and made his exitus."

Aside from the fact that these words could probably have been written only by a physician, they also capture the fatalism that was even more pronounced by the time of our meeting in November. Percy knew that there would not be many more trips to the Mayo Clinic and so very little point in mastering the machine whose parts lay scattered across the dining table. Out of some obdurate desire to put a cheerful face on things, I offered to turn the machine on and explain, as best I could, how it worked. He humored me in my efforts for perhaps a minute before walking a few steps to a nearby sofa and plopping down.

I proceeded to prattle on, but his indifference was formidable. There was something almost Olympian about it, an otherworldly indifference, though it was betrayed by the faintest hint of a smile—amusement, perhaps, at the futility of my efforts.

Soon I gave up and moved to his side of the room, taking a seat next to the sofa. He started talking about the Mayo Clinic—the difficulty of the journey, the treatment, the doctors. Coming to the last, he suddenly grew animated, his tone somewhere between bemused and irritated.

"You know something," he said, "not one of those doctors up there had read anything I've written. Not one of them had the least idea of who I was or what I did. The only person who recognized my name was a medical technician, and he asked for an autograph. I tell you one thing for sure: doctors don't read a damn thing."

It was possible to read a range of emotions in that short but animated explosion: irritation, amusement, punctured vanity. There was something else, too: disappointment. He was disappointed because the fraternity had let him down. Not that he honestly expected all doctors to be avid readers of his books. He knew better. He appreciated the demands of time on most physicians, and he understood that a practical turn of mind made most of them impatient readers of literature, at best. Still, it bothered him on those trips to Minnesota to encounter so many physicians who went through their busy lives untouched by the flame of literature. To him, that spoke of an incompleteness among the members of the fraternity to which he had once belonged—a failure to fulfill the potential of the doctorly ideal that he harbored.

In notes he kept in the early 1950s, not too long after he decided to abandon medicine for reasons having to do largely but not exclusively with health, Percy made an observation that suggests quite clearly how, and how much, he idealized the profession: "Doctors are a good lot. One cannot help thinking of them organized in a sort of medieval guild where their good qualities, the latent Christianity, might be fostered."

This revealing comment takes us very close to Percy's deepest feelings about the profession that he trained for, briefly entered, and then abandoned —or at least seemed to abandon. Percy joked quite often in his later years that he knew about as much medicine as any careful reader of *Reader's Digest.* But his claim was untrue on several counts, minor and major. He retained a great deal of technical knowledge, particularly from the two specialties, psychiatry and pathology, to which he had been drawn, and he remained more than passingly aware of developments within many medical fields. Readers of his books can certainly see how freely he drew on the medical lexicon. It appears in his close anatomical descriptions and in the dialogue of his physician characters. More profoundly, though, he had a physician's way of looking at people and their conditions—that is, at the sum of their physical, psychological, social, and spiritual conditions adding up to their whole human condition. He had a diagnostic manner and approach. For all his protestations to the contrary, he could never quite stop being a physician. He was a reluctant physician, and all the better, I would argue, for his reluctance.

The ambivalence goes back to Percy's reasons for choosing a medical career, although "reasons" might not be the precise word. Do we really mean "reasons" when we speak of the deep motivations that incline a person toward a career? Probably not. We are probably talking about the factors that go into the formation of the individual, the career or careers of the parents or grandparents or near relatives, the myths and legends that circulate through the household, the expectations laid on the child, the big life-shaping events that are sometimes of a physically or psychologically traumatic nature.

Nothing in Percy's earliest, preteen years would suggest an inclination toward medicine. He was bookish and solitary. His father, a Birmingham lawyer (and a descendant of other attorneys), passed on to his oldest son a love of literature and a fascination with aviation. There was a somewhat mysterious great uncle in the family's past who had been a doctor—one of three brothers who had settled in the wilds of the Mississippi Delta in the frontier days of the early nineteenth century—but he had come to a somewhat inglorious end, with a possible laudanum addiction. Yet it is doubtful this man figured in Walker's stock of acquired family lore.

The first step toward his eventual career, and, I believe, the decisive motivation, was his father's suicide, which occurred when Walker was thirteen years old. Not only was he stunned and saddened, as he later said, but he was angry and determined to make "damned sure" that what had happened to his father, and his grandfather, would not happen to him. The motive was powerful but problematic, bound up with the dark forces that haunted the Percy family, and the way in which he responded to it lies at the heart of his intellectual and literary achievements.

The next step toward medicine was Percy's great romance with science. It began in Greenville, Mississippi, in the house of William Alexander Percy, where the three Percy boys and their mother went a year after Leroy Percy's suicide. Uncle Will, as the boys called their cousin, formally adopted them after their mother died in a tragic and mysterious car accident.

Will Percy was a romantic figure—a decorated war veteran, a poet, a lawyer, a man whom everyone visiting the South wanted to meet. He was also a man of impeccable probity who held to an exacting Stoic code of conduct. He was, the boys always said, the best teacher they ever had.

Yet though Walker Percy was brought up through his adolescence in this most literary of households, he began to lean, perhaps partly in rebellion against his adoptive father, toward the world of science. This, we must remember, was at a time when science still seemed capable of anything and everything. (As Binx Bolling of *The Moviegoer* observes, "it was the nineteen thirties and everybody believed in science and talked about the ductless glands.") Percy read—imbibed is more the word—*The Science of Life* by H. G. Wells and Julian Huxley, taking to heart its great, almost hubristic confidence that all life's mysteries could be solved through the techniques of science. This heady brand of scientism was given further dramatic coloring by another book that Percy read as a teenager, Sinclair Lewis's *Arrowsmith*. As well as satirizing Lewis's favorite target, the philistine values of middle-class America, the novel celebrates the new field of scientific medical research. Its eponymous hero is torn between being an old-fashioned "doc" and following in the footsteps of a great medical researcher, Max Gottlieb, a character patterned closely after the famous Jacques Loeb of the Rockefeller Institute. The figure of Gottlieb/Loeb seems similarly to have inspired young Percy, perhaps even influencing his choice of medical school, Columbia's College of Physicians and Surgeons, as well as his specialty, pathology. Columbia was reputed, along with Johns Hopkins and Harvard, to be at the forefront of investigative medicine, a strongly scientific, research-oriented approach that came from Germany largely by way of New York's Rockefeller Institute. Pathology, at least in Percy's view, was the most scientific of the specialties, though he claims that he was also attracted to a very dissimilar specialty, psychiatry.

But disillusionment with the heroic ideal of scientific medicine started creeping in even before Percy entered medical school. As an undergraduate at the University of North Carolina, majoring in chemistry, Percy found himself wondering whether he had the scientific researcher's passion. His search had *something* to do with science—with its conjectural and analytic approach—but he kept being distracted from the objects of research. In *The Moviegoer,* we hear the clearest articulation of Percy's problem with pure scientific research. The speaker is Binx Bolling; Harry is his laboratory partner, a true researcher.

> I tried research one summer. I got interested in the role of acid-base balance in the formation of renal calculi; really, it's quite an interesting problem. . . . But then a peculiar thing happened. I became extraordinarily affected by the summer afternoons in the laboratory. The August sunlight came streaming in the great dusty fanlights and lay in yellow bars across the room. The old building ticked and creaked in the heat. . . . I became bewitched by the presence of the building; for minutes at a stretch I sat on the floor and watched the motes rise and fall in the sunlight. I called Harry's attention to the presence but he shrugged and went on with his work. He was absolutely unaffected by the singularities of time and place. His abode was anywhere. . . . Yet I do not envy him. I would not change places with him if he discovered the cause and cure of cancer. For he is no more aware of the mystery that surrounds him than a fish is aware of the water it swims in. He could do research for a thousand years and never have an inkling of it. By the middle of August I could not see what difference it made whether the pigs got kidney stones or not (they didn't, incidentally), compared to the mystery of those summer afternoons.

Now, we can make many things of this passage. For one, we can conclude that Binx—and by extension Percy himself—is a very self-absorbed fellow with an inflated notion of the value of his existential musings. Or we can think that Binx is indeed engaged in a higher pursuit. Neither conclusion is adequate to the ironic truth that Percy is attempting to dramatize here: the scientific method is a gloriously elegant tool for arriving at general truths about the workings of the physical world but a wholly inadequate instrument for dealing with the individual human being in relation to oneself, one's fellows, and one's world. The danger of the method (and this goes far beyond this passage to matters that Percy wrestled with in his philosophical and linguistic essays as well as in his other novels) is that it can affect its user, and indeed the entire culture that places an almost religious confidence in it, in such a way as to leave both abstracted from themselves: ghosts in the machine, minds separated not just from bodies but from selves. People who are blind to what makes them individuals—creatures in unique relation to the world and their fellows—are themselves suffering from a kind of illness, whose mechanism Percy was beginning only dimly to descry in the laboratories of Venable Hall during those long undergraduate afternoons at Chapel Hill.

Yet Percy did not abandon science. In fact, one could say that his great intellectual challenge was to bring the generalizing power of science to the problem of the individual's estrangement from himself. Many of Percy's critics argue that he never succeeded in meeting this challenge. Some charge that he remained too much a slave to the Cartesian dualism he was trying to overcome; others find little scientific validity in his anthropology, as he called his science of humanity, or in its foundational hypothesis about the uniqueness of human language.

Whether he succeeded or failed in his intellectual ambition, it is clear that Percy's early pursuit of a medical career helped situate him at the very center of the dialectic whose terms he would work and live through until the last of his days. I think his suspension between the objectivizing power of science and the particularizing power of art was evident even in his uncertainty about his choice of specialties: psychiatry drew him more toward what is unique about each human being; pathology, toward what is most universal. Although he settled on pathology, practicing it during the advanced stages of his treatment at a tuberculosis sanatorium and even briefly teaching it before the first of many relapses, his curiosity in psychiatry remained strong.

One reason it did was that Percy began to suffer from the same kind of sharp depressions that had tormented his father and grandfather. At medical school, to confront these darkening glooms, he underwent psychoanalysis, most of it with a gifted female practitioner, Dr. Janet Rioch, who was a disciple of Harry Stack Sullivan. This tie to Sullivan and his ideas proved crucial. A brilliant and unhappy man himself, Sullivan helped move psychoanalysis and psychotherapy away from a narrow preoccupation with fixed psychodynamic mechanisms of the kind on which Freud insisted toward a closer concern with the particularities—social, cultural, economic, and existential—of the individual case. It was a psychiatric approach from which Percy greatly benefited, intellectually as well as emotionally. It led him to an understanding not only of himself but of the culture and family that shaped him. Indeed, his fiction would in large measure be a vivid re-creation of the world he came out of—a comedic taming of the dark, tragic realities of his background. I don't want to overstate their therapeutic value at the expense of their solid artistic achievement, but Percy's novels were at least in part his physicianly means of healing himself.

But something is missing in these reflections on Percy's ties to the medical profession. It is perhaps the one thing that people who have only a vague awareness of Percy know: that he was a Catholic writer. That, along with the fact that he was southern. And so he is conveniently pigeonholed: a southern Catholic writer, like Flannery O'Connor.

Percy would have been immensely flattered by the comparison with that sharp and funny writer from Milledgeville, Georgia, but he knew that such broad-stroke comparisons ultimately avail very little. Their differences, he knew, were far more interesting than what they had in common. One difference was that Flannery O'Connor was a cradle Catholic, whereas Percy was a convert. (As one of Percy's friends used to say to him, "You wouldn't have become such a zealot if you had been whipped by the nuns.")

Percy's conversion to Catholicism is itself a complicated story. These are just a few of the biographical facts that lie behind it, in no order of causal importance: one, he was born and raised in his early years in a very liberal Presbyterian church; two, there was little churchgoing in the house of Uncle Will, who himself had once been a very devout, indeed pious, Roman Catholic, but had abandoned it all as an undergraduate; three, beginning in high school, Percy was known for his extreme cynicism, his almost aggressive agnosticism, which seemed to go hand in hand with his allegiance to science; four, in college, medical school, and even the sanatorium, he formed close connections with Catholics who almost uniformly impressed him with the seriousness of their convictions, even while he argued with them and made fun of them; five, while in the sanatorium, he began to read Catholic thinkers, including Aquinas, and other religious thinkers such as Kierkegaard; six, he always seemed to be in search of authority, whether of a political or philosophical nature; seven, he first confessed his interest in Catholicism to his friend Shelby Foote while they were in New Mexico in 1946 (Foote responding with the charge that Percy's mind was clearly "in full intellectual retreat"); eight, he took his first steps toward conversion shortly after his marriage in 1947, his wife accompanying him; nine, he remained a Catholic, though not without periods of doubt and near-apostasy, until his death.

All these facts—and perhaps many others—are important details in Percy's spiritual journey, but what we are concerned with here is the relationship between that journey and his reluctant standing as a physician. The connection, I believe, is suggested in the note from the early 1950s in which Percy wrote that doctors were basically a "good lot" who should still be organized in "a sort of medieval guild where their good qualities, the latent Christianity, might be fostered."

What he was talking about was in part simple historical fact: medicine, in the medieval educational and professional system, was, like law, a branch of the clerisy. But even in the pagan or pre-Christian cultures of the West, particularly the Greek, medicine always had a strong spiritual component. So much are we children of the scientific worldview that we have lost an appreciation of how thoroughly medicine was integrated into a full philosophical-religious system dedicated to the well-being of the whole human being. For all its primitivisms, from leeching to bleeding to humor theory, medieval and ancient doctors at their best kept their eye on the object of their skills more vigilantly than modern science does. For all the blessings of specialization and the scientific and technological wizardry of modern medicine, its bane has been a diminished connection between the physician and the patient—and a loss, perhaps, of a clear vision of the overall objective.

Percy, according to those who witnessed him in training, had a good bedside manner, a knack for dealing with all patients, for that matter. He zeroed in on people; he listened intently; he showed good diagnostic judgment, but he never lost sight of the patient. Yet what Percy himself remembered most about working with patients was how exhausting it was. This undoubtedly had much to do with his own frail psychological and physical health. He was never a robust person. At the same time, though, I think some of his exhaustion stemmed from his resistance to the kind of depersonalized doctor-patient relationship that the modern medical training seems to foster, if not demand.

To be sure, depersonalization in some medical situations, such as surgery, is healthy and even necessary. Yet in others, perhaps in most others, it is a symptom of a dehumanized, demoralized, dispirited profession. Melvin Konner, in his valuable book *Becoming a Doctor* (which should be required reading in all medical schools), shows that modern medical education cultivates this depersonalization to such an extent that even the most idealistically motivated students feel defeated. It is not a healthy state of affairs, as doubtless every physician knows; nor ultimately is it separable from the larger health-care crisis this nation faces. Among other things, the excessive scientization of medicine has led people to expect medicine to cure anything and everything. And because physicians do not see their patients as humans, patients have reciprocated.

This may seem to be drifting away from Walker Percy. It is not. Percy, I believe, felt deeply frustrated by the gap between the potential and the reality of modern medicine—and by the physician's lot within it. His frustration and abiding concern are evident in many ways, including in work he did on a schizophrenia project in the 1970s, which dealt very much with the problematic relationship between the doctor and the patient, but nowhere more vividly than in his novels, particularly those featuring physicians either as protagonists or important characters. From his unpublished apprentice novel, *The Gramercy Winner* (where two very different doctors in a sanatorium play a crucial part in the protagonist's spiritual awakening), to his last novel, *The Thanatos Syndrome,* the key physician characters are troubled figures of authority. Their one advantage over the more contentedly tucked-away physicians is that they know they are in trouble.

Even the wretchedly cynical Sutter Vaught in *The Last Gentleman,* who knows that he is bad news and repeatedly warns the confused seeker protagonist of the novel, Will Barrett, to steer clear of him, is still able to offer up his own mishandled authority as a guidepost to what Barrett should avoid. Sutter Vaught represents at least one of the virtues of the medical intelligence: an unflinching awareness of mortality, shorn of all cheaply reassuring sentimental notions. Although he is a monster of rationality, he recognizes, in spite of himself, that the truth of the flesh alone is inadequate. Taunting his sister, a nun, he reveals the pain of his own spiritual dryness, and despite his raging cynicism, he in the most subtle of ways aids a priest in the last-minute baptism of his dying brother. The deathbed scene at the end of the novel is crucial because it hints so delicately at the lost world of collaboration between physical and spiritual caretakers: in this moment, the bonds of a lost fraternity—the fraternity that Percy idealized—are almost restored.

The physician today, like everyone else in the modern world, works very much in isolation. Such fellowship as exists among physicians, at least after the rigors of school and internships where battlefield bonds are made, is founded almost exclusively on the technicalities of shared specialties. It is not so much solidarity as shoptalk. And the condition of solitude heightens the cynicism and selfishness that is so often associated with physicians today. It was to combat the cynicism and selfishness in himself—emotions that fueled his psychological depression and his spiritual despair—that Percy turned with earnestness to the Christian faith, with its emphasis on self-abnegation and love of one's fellows. But faith, for Percy, was less an attained state than an ongoing struggle, and the finest literary representation of that struggle is the character of Tom More, protagonist of both *Love in the Ruins* and *The Thanatos Syndrome.*

In the first of these novels, Dr. More is, in fact, very much Percy's self-parody: a scientist who is trying to devise a machine, an ontological lapsometer, not only to measure but to overcome humankind's dividedness. In a rich satire of everything that has run amok in the modern world, from Knothead conservatism to liberal Pollyannaism, from psychobabble to sex therapy clinics, from golf tournaments to Christ for Property Rights Sundays, Percy lampoons nothing more sharply than his own ambitions. "The Adventures of a Bad Catholic at a Time near the End of the World" is the novel's subtitle, and the lesson that the hero comes to is that dividedness is nothing that humanity alone, through intellection or invention, can solve. Attempting to do so, as More demonstrates, is to fall deeper into the despair that already threatens to crush him. The only way up for the near-alcoholic doctor is to be thrown down even farther; the only way to rejoin his fellows is to be cast utterly apart. As for More, so for the community in which he lives: it must go to ruins before a new community, a true community, can be built. There can be no cure until there is a crisis—a truth of medicine as well.

It sounds like the rankest of clichés to say that Percy discovered that the best medicine is laughter. Yet this is the case no more for Percy than for any other writer identified as writing from a religious position—from Dante and Chaucer to O'Connor and Waugh, from the authors of the books of the Bible through Saul Bellow and Cynthia Ozick. Comedy is the literary expression of faith, of hope for things unseen, a gift that can infuse the seen world with a life that is otherwise lacking. As a physician in spite of himself, Percy brought the diagnostic method to literary and philosophical analysis. (He brought semiotics, the science of signs, from medicine as well.) Moreover, as a believing Christian, he brought the healing power of a comic vision to his own form of doctoring. This vision has both diagnostic and prescriptive values: it serves in pointing out our follies and vanities not simply to ridicule them but to remind us of our illness and incompleteness, of our need for each other, and, possibly, of an animating power beyond our seeing. Percy was a reluctant physician because he found the terms of doctoring in our time too narrow, even deadening. Yet he never truly quit the guild. Instead, he went about doctoring in his own way, even while reminding his fellow physicians what "good qualities" their guild should foster.

Afterword: Writing and Rewriting Stories

John Lantos

The essays in this volume speak to Walker Percy's influence on many people. Some of the physician-authors see Percy's message as central and important to their work as healers or teachers. Others see Percy's message as much more general, concerned not only with medicine but with life. For Percy, questions that are central to medicine, such as how we deal with suffering and how we care for sufferers, go well beyond medicine. They are life's spiritual challenges, and doctors have developed one particular response. But everyone must try to describe and make sense of the situations in which they find themselves. When the suffering seems unbearable, how do we decide whether and how to go on? Why does an individual life matter?

One of the more intriguing themes in Percy's work, and in these responses, is the dynamic tension between medicine and storytelling. Although he gave up being a practicing physician, Percy clearly continued to be influenced and informed by something connected to medicine, its sense of mission, its unique gaze. His medical years were not wasted. He saw his novels as "diagnostic" exercises; many of his protagonists were physicians, and his "foil" was often the scientific worldview of modern medicine and its inadequacy to larger religious or metaphysical questions.

Percy was not a systematic thinker. He returned again and again to certain themes, but mostly to play with them, reformulate questions, tell stories that suggested responses and forced readers to respond. In a Percyesque fashion, we might try to "diagnose" the man himself, and to understand why he turned away from the formal practice of medicine and toward storytelling as a way of addressing his concerns about how we care for one another. I have a hunch. To explain my hunch, I need to tell a story of my own.

In my own pediatric practice, I was consulted recently about a young girl—call her Jane—who had sickle-cell disease. She also had a serious eating disorder. She was sent to my hospital because we have a program that specializes in the care of children who have sickle-cell disease. I was the attending physician on the inpatient service during the month that she was admitted. Because of this arrangement, neither the patient nor her parents chose me as their doctor, and I would not be responsible for their primary care once Jane was discharged from the hospital. Instead, they would go back to their HMO and their primary-care pediatrician.

Because of my concern about her eating disorder, I recommended to Jane's parents that she see a psychiatrist. The parents were not eager to have her do this, and their HMO was not eager to pay for it, in spite of my repeated attempts to convince both of them that psychiatric evaluation was urgent. There was something quite threatening to them all about the possibility that Jane's disease might be more than physical, and that the only treatment might be the sort of self-examination that old-fashioned psychotherapy demanded. Neither the parents nor the HMO were unique in these views.

Throughout medicine today runs a deep suspicion and distrust of the sort of healing that psychotherapy represents. To a certain extent, it is a distrust of the human aspect of healing, the power of a doctor-patient relationship that does not rely on the intercession of biochemical or radiological or surgical intervention. In our suspicion of this human aspect of healing, we aspire to a medicine that does not depend on the individual healer or the idiosyncratic efforts and ideas of the patient. That sort of medicine, we argue, hasn't been scientifically validated, is not cost-effective, does not have a neurochemical or molecular genetic basis. If it works, or when it works, we can't imagine why. It challenges most of the pragmatic paradigms that exert such a strong moral force on medicine today.

In his last book, *The Thanatos Syndrome,* Percy's protagonist, Tom More, is an old-fashioned psychiatrist. Many of his patients seem to have improved much more as a result of a new psychotropic drug than they did as a result of years of psychotherapy. Their anxieties disappear, their marriages seem happier, they no longer want or need his help. Dr. More is confused. Are they better? Are his skills, intuitions, and interventions obsolete? Dr. More may be Percy's alter ego, a physician who realizes that talking cures are more properly the realm of literature than medicine, and the doctor who practices them should more appropriately write stories than take care of patients.

My patient needed someone to whom she could tell her story, carefully, painstakingly; someone who could listen carefully and analyze both the content and the gaps, the hesitations, the tremors of her voice, and the suppressed tears. But she would not get that. Her parents never took her to see the psychiatrist. Her primary pediatrician supported that decision. Together, they agreed that there was nothing more to be done except repeated admissions to the hospital for intravenous narcotics to control the abdominal pain that everybody insisted on seeing as related only to her red blood cells.

I was angry at both the parents and the doctors, disappointed and discouraged by my own inefficacy. It seemed as if there was nothing that I could do. But that wasn't quite right. In my powerlessness, I decided to write Jane's story, disguising her enough to preserve confidentiality, but describing her accurately enough so that someday, if she or her parents should happen on her story, they might recognize it and perhaps even be moved to rewrite it.

Perhaps some similar combination of anger and powerlessness motivated Percy to seek a path of healing that relied less on cures for suffering and more on telling the stories of those who suffer. Compared to penicillin, it ain't much, but for some really tough cases, it may be all we've got.

Contributors

Robert Coles is the James Agee Professor of Social Ethics and professor of psychiatry and medical humanities at Harvard University. He is the author of many books, including *Walker Percy: An American Search* and most recently *Old and on Their Own*. He won the Pulitzer Prize in 1972 for his book series, Children of Crisis.

Brock Eide is an attending physician in the Department of Internal Medicine at Provident Hospital of Cook County (Chicago) and a doctoral candidate in the Committee on Social Thought at the University of Chicago. He has published in fields ranging from clinical medicine and molecular biology to medical ethics and the medical humanities. His doctoral thesis is on moral psychology in the novels of Fyodor Dostoyevsky.

Carl Elliott is an expatriate South Carolinian living in Minneapolis. He teaches bioethics and philosophy at the University of Minnesota, and his books include *A Philosophical Disease: Bioethics, Culture, and Identity* and *The Rules of Insanity: Moral Responsibility and Mental Illness*. He has lived and taught in Scotland, New Zealand, South Africa, and Quebec.

John Lantos is Chief of the Section of General Pediatrics and Associate Director of the MacLean Center for Clinical Medical Ethics at the University of Chicago. He is the author of *Do We Still Need Doctors?* and the forthcoming *Pound of Flesh: Preemies and Public Policy*. He lives in Chicago with his wife and three daughters.

Ross McElwee's autobiographical documentary trilogy comprises three feature films, *Sherman's March, Time Indefinite,* and *Six O'Clock News*. Originally from North Carolina, he now lives in Brookline, Massachusetts, and teaches filmmaking in Harvard University's Department of Visual and Environmental Studies.

Richard Martinez completed undergraduate studies at Tulane University, completed a master of humanities degree at the University of Colorado, and received his M.D. from LSU Medical School in New Orleans. At Harvard Medical School, he completed a fellowship in the Division of Medical Ethics (1994–1995), followed by a fellowship in the Program in Ethics and the Professions at Harvard University (1995–1996). He is an Assistant Professor in the Program in Health Care Ethics, Humanities, and Law and in the Department of Psychiatry at the University of Colorado Health Sciences Center.

Martha Montello is Assistant Professor of History and Philosophy of Medicine at the University of Kansas School of Medicine. She teaches and writes curriculum in narrative ethics and medical humanities. She has previously written on Walker Percy for *The New Orleans Review*.

David Schiedermayer practices general internal medicine at the primary care clinic of the Medical College of Wisconsin. He has authored and coauthored many papers and books focusing on the doctor-patient relationship, spirituality in medicine, and medical ethics. His latest book is a poetry collection, *House Calls, Rounds, and Healings*. He has an interest in the medical care of the underserved, and part of his medical training occurred in Liberia, West Africa, at ELWA hospital. He also took a sabbatical at Tuba City hospital on the western Navajo reservation in Arizona.

Jay Tolson, the editor of *The Wilson Quarterly*, is the author of *Pilgrim in the Ruins: A Life of Walker Percy* and editor of *The Correspondence of Shelby Foote and Walker Percy*.

Bertram Wyatt-Brown is Richard J. Milbauer Professor of History, University of Florida, and is the author of *Southern Honor: Ethics and Behavior in the Old South; The House of Percy: Honor, Melancholy, and Imagination in a Southern Family; The Literary Percys: Family History, Gender, and Legend,* and other works.

Laurie Zoloth is Associate Professor of Social Ethics and Director of the Program in Jewish Studies at San Francisco State University. She is also cofounder of the Ethics Practice, a group that has provided bioethics consultation and education services to health care providers and health care systems nationally. Zoloth has worked as a nurse for twenty years in the fields of perinatology and neonatal intensive care. She is the coeditor, with Dena Davis, of *Notes from a Narrow Ridge: Religion and Bioethics,* and with Susan Rubin, of *Margin of Error: The Necessity, Inevitability, and Ethics of Mistakes in Medicine and Bioethics Consultation.*

Index

Library of Congress Cataloging-in-Publication Data
The last physician : Walker Percy and the moral life of medicine / edited by
Carl Elliott and John Lantos.
   p.   cm.
Includes index.
ISBN 0-8223-2336-2 (alk. paper). — ISBN 0-8223-2369-9 (pbk. : alk. paper)
1. Percy, Walker, 1916- —Criticism and interpretation.   2. Literature and
mental illness—United States—History— 20th century.   3. Literature and
medicine—United States— History—20th century.   4. Physicians' writings,
American—History and criticism.   5. Percy, Walker, 1916- —Knowledge—
Medicine.   6. Percy, Walker, 1916- —Ethics.   7. Medicine in literature.
8. Ethics in literature.   9. Medical ethics.   I. Elliott, Carl.   II. Lantos, John D.
PS3566.E6912Z738   1999
813'.54—dc21
                                                                        99-14158
                                                                            CIP